MW00578680

# 100 ESSENTIAL CDs

## THE ROUGH GUIDE

There are more than one hundred and fifty Rough Guide travel, phrasebook, and music titles, covering destinations from Amsterdam to Zimbabwe, languages from Czech to Thai, and musics from World to Opera and Jazz

### Other 100 Essential CD titles

Classical Music • Opera • Reggae

### Rough Guides on the Internet

www.roughguides.com

## Rough Guide Credits

Text editor: Greg Ward
Series editor: Mark Ellingham
Typesetting: Helen Ostick

## Publishing Information

This first edition published September 1999 by
Rough Guides Ltd, 62–70 Shorts Gardens, London, WC2H 9AB

**Distributed by the Penguin Group:**

Penguin Books Ltd, 27 Wrights Lane, London W8 5TZ
Penguin Books USA Inc., 375 Hudson Street, New York 10014, USA
Penguin Books Australia Ltd, 487 Maroondah Highway,
PO Box 257, Ringwood, Victoria 3134, Australia
Penguin Books Canada Ltd, 10 Alcorn Avenue,
Toronto, Ontario, Canada M4V 1E4
Penguin Books (NZ) Ltd, 182–190 Wairau Road,
Auckland 10, New Zealand

Typeset in Bembo and Helvetica to an original design by Henry Iles.
Printed in Spain by Graphy Cems.

© Al Spicer
208pp

A catalogue record for this book is available from the British Library.
**ISBN 1-85828-490-2**

# Rock

## 100 ESSENTIAL CDs

### THE ROUGH GUIDE

**by Al Spicer**

# Contents List

# Introduction

The Rough Guide to Essential Rock CDs is not just another list of the "Greatest Rock Albums Ever Made" – it's a guide that packs the whole story of rock into just two hundred pages, celebrating the best albums by one hundred bands and artists, ranging from the zillion-sellers to the wilfully obscure. The expected "All-Time Greats" are here, but more deeply buried gems are keeping them company: Elvis, Joni Mitchell, Madonna, the Beatles and the Stones get their entries, along with the likes of Bikini Kill, PJ Harvey, Sleater-Kinney, Tortoise, Jeff Buckley and Aphex Twin.

It was of course hellishly hard to select a mere hundred records from the countless number released each year for the last thirty years. We began with a list of all the indisputably classic acts and all those we think have in some way pushed back the limits, taking the music into uncharted lands. The job of cutting this initial batch of nearly one thousand was made a little easier by the decision to bring out Rough Guide Essentials devoted to Soul, Blues, Reggae and Country, but even so, many long after-noons and arguments were spent trimming down the huge list: who was it to be – Frank Zappa or the Cramps? Suede or the Kinks? In the end, by limiting even the biggest names to a single album, plus an alternative recommendation at the end of the review, we believe we've come up with a handbook that encom-passes every shade of rock. The bulk of the recordings come from the 70s and 80s, the "Golden Age" of the rock 'n' roll album, a time before the sheer volume of releases made it impos-sible for any one person to keep fully up to date with everything that went by the name of rock music. We've given the origina-tors their due as well, peeking into the 50s and taking a closer look at the 60s explosion. And we've stuck our necks out by recommending the pick of the 90s.

So, this is a book of the boppiest, brainiest, scariest, dumbest, loudest, most sincere, most skilfully executed, most sloppily per-formed recordings by the glammest, saddest, quietest and noisiest performers of the last three decades. Recorded at the highest-tech palaces, live in concert or during snatched half-hours in backstreet studios by artists and producers with hugely differing intentions and levels of ability, all these recordings have one single thing in common; they are each, in their own way, marvellous and life-changing.

## Acknowledgements

Firstly I'd like to thank the Rough Guides crew – Jonathan Buckley, Martin "The Hawk" Dunford and Mark Ellingham for their advice and support, Helen "Insomniac" Ostick for the 140 b.p.m. typesetting and faultless musical taste, and Charlotte Marriott for her ceaseless dedication and countless hours spent on the project.

Next up, a big shout to Greg Ward for his classy editing, sense of humour and ability to extract coherence from my ramblings, and to my fellow contributors Chris Coe, Richard Fontenoy, Jason Gross, Andrew Rosenberg and Peter Shapiro.

My love and heartfelt thanks go to Jane Holly for endless patience and assistance, and to George, Bustina and Tallulah for their help with the typing.

Finally, to everybody who made suggestions and offered criticism, you can stop now, the book's written.

Al Spicer

# AC/DC

## Back in Black

Atlantic, 1980

Angus Young (gtr), Malcolm Young (gtr), Brian Johnson (vocals), Cliff Williams (bass), Phil Rudd (drums).

Some people never tire of proclaiming that rock'n'roll is about one thing, and one thing only: youth culture in all of its silly, misunderstood, inarticulate, cocksure glory. If that's true, then **Back in Black** is the greatest rock album of all time. A collection of ribaldry to make Chaucer and Petronius blush, it's packed with locker-room tales of wild sex which never happened, Neanderthal relationship politics, and odes to wine and song that are far more affectionate than odes to women. Not even Chuck Berry has painted so portrait of the male adolescent experience.

*Back in Black* is much more than just a blitzing of teen curity in a flurry of hoary old dick-as-weapon meta also a resilient testament to the life-affirming power o 'n'roll lifestyle, in the face of an equally powerful n destruction. *Back in Black* was the first AC/DC alb previous lead singer, Bon Scott, choked to dea booze-induced vomit in February 1980. Replac Brian Johnson, the mainstays of the band, bro Malcolm Young, crafted a stockpile of rock cli tic, galvanizing album that celebrated the Rolling Stones-style debauchery, despite the themselves were by now bloated tax exil since exposed by punk.

Above all, what makes *Back in Black* the magnum opus of hard rock is the almighty power of the riff. None of the many guitarists who have swiped licks from Keith Richards and Jimmy Page has done so more effectively – or more shamelessly – than Angus and Malcolm Young. Both the title track, Back in Black itself, and Shake a Leg are explosions of relentless forward motion that encapsulate the very essence of rock, with an impact to match "Whole Lotta Love" and "Black Dog". It might seem blasphemous to say so, but on You Shook Me All Night Long the Youngs out-Keef Keef himself, inspiring in the process more back-seat gropes than anything this side of Motown. Rock and Roll Ain't Noise Pollution may not be as great a claim of immortality as the Showmen's classic "It Will Stand", but it does feature the marvellously dumb but undeniable truth: "Rock and roll ain't no pollution / Rock and roll is just rock and roll."

In addition, AC/DC eulogize their lost vocalist, with fitting gallows humour, on tracks like Hells' Bells ("You're only young, but you're going to die"), Have a Drink on Me, which remains the national anthem for burn-outs everywhere, and "Back in Black" ("Forget the hearse because I'll never die / I've got nine lives, cat's eyes"). The album only loses its way in the misjudged attempts to match Scott's bawdy, back-room tales like Shoot to Thrill, What Do You Do For Money Honey, and Let Me Put My Love Into You, which merely succeed in ⁀ing as stupid as you'd guess from their titles.

The glorious interaction between monolithic riffage and Phil 'd's drums on "Back in Black" and "You Shook Me" is s to the genius who defined the sound of Eighties stadium master producer Robert John "Mutt" Lange. Many scholars consider Lange's production too clean, com-that by rendering the bass virtually inaudible, and damp-drums so they don't crack your ribs the way they used stripped things down to the raw, crisp essentials. re the riffs, which do everything that rock demands: ke names later.

chose **Dirty Deeds Done Dirt Cheap**, Atlantic, 1976

# Aphex Twin

## Richard D. James Album

WARP, 1996

Richard D. James (all instruments and production).

Under the pseudonym of Aphex Twin, Richard D James has created his own unique niche in the world of electronica, and established himself as one of the UK's most innovative musicians. On the eponymous **Richard D James Album**, his peculiar vision was responsible for a matchless creation of moods, from almost-traditional rock'n'roll band grooves to collages of breakbeats sewn so closely together that they appear as single tones.

The archetypal guy-in-a-bedroom, home-studio obsessive, James grew up and developed his music in the comparative isolation of Cornwall in the far west of England. In the mid-Eighties, when he made his first experimental recordings, neither electronic nor dance music were widely carried by the mainstream radio or record outlets to which he had access. It was this enforced distance from the trends then emerging in Bristol, Manchester, London and elsewhere, that made Aphex Twin's work so intriguing. His music is far more artful, and far more cleverly constructed, than the "rustic craftsman" image he so assiduously promotes might suggest. To generate the precise combination of emotions that he requires, each note – each and every tone or individually compressed, equalized and pitch-shifted beat – has to be selected and electronically tweaked.

James picked up his first radio play through jungle/drum'n'bass DJ Colin Dale's show on London's Kiss FM station, and jungle's original vocabulary of sub-bass frequencies, rudely assembled shards of percussion, and distressed melodies, was to form the bedrock of his work. On both the opening track of the *Richard D James Album*, 4, and Cornmouth, which ends its "first side", beats jar and shudder together, while cheap-sounding keyboards contribute difficult atonal melodies. A lighter, more spacious feeling is added by the sudden unexpected stops – pauses far too short to catch breath – that punch holes in the mix. En route to its stun-effect power ending, "Cornmouth" also boasts sections of fearsome electronic noise, overwhelming machine-gun-percussive chords, and chiming keyboard effects.

An unsettling humour permeates the entire album. On Cornish Acid, for example, the enfeebled offspring of the classic "squelch and squiggle" keyboard sound of acid house toddles precariously atop an impossible drumbeat stitched from badly matched fragments. To Cure A Weakling Child – which also showed up on the *Come To Daddy* mini-LP – features children's voices cut up and re-assembled to follow a singing-teacher's piano line. That simple tune is then pasted onto wild, totally unconnected breakbeats that shimmer to the front of the mix, fade out slowly, and burst back in before mutating away in a welter of incongruous noise.

Peek 824545801 shows James at his boffin-like best. Bursts of modulated data are used as melodies, frequencies are twisted to resemble taut wires under rainstorms, and bleeps reverberate and ricochet through a landscape of junglist, industrial noise before, as if bored with the direction of the music, the tape recorder is switched off, and runs down slowly to a halt.

As advertising commissions pile up at his door, Richard James can afford to keep on upgrading his equipment, adding to his enormous stock of samples, and stumbling, eyes tightly shut and gleeful, down the unknown path of his choosing. By all accounts rendered no weirder by success than he was in the first place, he continues to produce absorbing, high-quality soundtracks to films that remain as yet unscripted.

➲ We almost chose **Selected Ambient Works Vol 2**, Warp, 1995

# Bad Brains

## Bad Brains

ROIR, 1982

Dr Know (born Gary Miller, gtr), H.R. (born Paul D. Hudson, vocals), Darryl Aaron Jennifer (bass), Earl Hudson (drums).

With their force-fed insertion of the millennial fervour of reggae into the visceral immediacy of hardcore, no one has ever chanted down Babylon with the ferocity of Washington DC's Bad Brains. Professionals in a genre that celebrated amateurism, Rastafarians who made music for an audience who believed in nothing but nihilism, blacks in a scene that was otherwise one hundred percent white, Bad Brains never exactly endeared themselves to the hardcore community, but their self-titled first album (originally a cassette-only release on New York's ROIR label) remains perhaps the genre's finest hour.

Bad Brains started out as a jazz-fusion band called Mind Power. However, sucker-punched by punk rock, they soon ditched the Al DiMeola licks, re-named themselves after a track from the Ramones' *Road to Ruin*, and dove headfirst into DC's nascent hardcore scene. After being blacklisted from the capital's clubs thanks to homophobic remarks, the band moved to New York, where they recorded **Bad Brains** in the summer of 1981.

From the very first track, Sailin' On, you know this is no ordinary bleat of adolescent spleen. Though Earl Hudson thwacks his drum kit like a jackhammer, Darryl Jennifer lays down a crunching one-note bassline, and Dr Know riffs away in overdrive, the thrash is lightened by high-pitched vocal hooks and the faintest hint of a melody. Just as you start to wonder if these guys are soft, however, Don't Need It, with vocalist H.R.'s declamatory rasping, leaps out like the Lion of Judah. The joyous refrain of Attitude – "We got that attitude / Hey we got the P.M.A." (positive mental attitude) – makes it clear there's more going down than merely venting aggression at the high school bully or the head cheerleader.

*Bad Brains'* best songs bristle with a righteous Rastafarian rage, while the heavy metal thunder is peppered with sufferer's chants like Leaving Babylon and I Luv I Jah, and the dub of Jah Calling – the living incarnation of Bob Marley's "Punky Reggae Party". In the US, however – unlike in England – reggae and hardcore did not go hand in hand, and the band remained prophets without honour, whose spirituality and willingness to expand the conventions of the genre alienated hardcore purists.

That said, although Bad Brains' reggae moves give you a chance to catch your breath, the mangled metal mayhem is what makes this the essential hardcore document. The band's instrumental prowess meant they understood the power of the riff better than their hardcore contemporaries. On I, Dr. Know perfectly blends the pomp of heavy metal with the frenzy of punk, while the chorus sounds like Judas Priest being cheered on by The Business. Big Take Over seems to argue against the very miscegenation on which Bad Brains' career was based, but its heart-attack chords and hand-clap beat blow any such worries away after the first bar.

The crowning glory of the album, however, is a re-recording of Pay to Cum, which had been Bad Brains' first single in 1980. One of the fastest records ever made, it remains hardcore's ultimate anthem, and its greatest ode to the cathartic power of speed. Atop an utterly majestic guitar riff, and a rhythm section caught in a 250-bpm tumble cycle, H.R. tries to enunciate lines like "I make decisions with precision" and "In this world we all must pay / Pay to write, pay to play, pay to cum, pay to fight". The end result is what journalist Sasha Frere-Jones hailed as "the hardest hardcore ever".

➲ We almost chose **I Against I**, SST, 1986

# Bauhaus

## Press The Eject And Give Me The Tape

Beggars Banquet, 1982/1988

Peter Murphy (vocals), Daniel Ash (gtr), David Jay (bass), Kevin Haskins (drums).

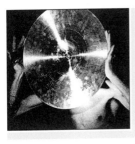

Tall, gaunt, dangerously thin and perilously good-looking, Bauhaus epitomized the sheer, fiendish glee of early Goth in the UK. Before people began drinking blood, conjuring up demons and taking the whole thing far too seriously, came a few golden years of genuine fascination with myth and fantasy, coupled of course with pounding, ritualistic, drum-led music for pale white kids to dance to. The Bauhaus blend of camp B-movie horror and ambivalent sexuality worked best on stage, in front of an audience, where Murphy's monochrome take on Bowie's Ziggy Stardust persona could break the hearts of the four front rows, and Ash's guitar lightning flash through the hall, while the Jay/Haskins team provided the thunder.

**Press The Eject And Give Me The Tape** captures the band in all its live glory, in a series of gigs in London, Liverpool, Manchester and Paris. Of its two versions of In The Flat Field, title track to their first album, the second, recorded in Paris, is clearly the stronger performance, though the recording itself is unfortunately muffled. Both, however, convey a sense of massive power, barely held in check, with guitar feedback howling like a banshee, immense drum attack, and terrifying bass. The brooding fear multiplies on Rose Garden Funeral Of Sores, a John Cale track, where Murphy's full star-vocal treatment soars over the insistent, mechanical-sounding rhythm section. This Gothic re-working of the old "Shakin' All Over" riff gains menace from the Eighties-trademark SynDrum, treated bass guitar tones, and the two frantic, screaming voices that call it to a halt. The Man With X-Ray Eyes has an equally merciless feel, its distorted bass and guitar notes held on sustain almost beyond endurance. Lines like "Wipe away my eyes, I have seen too much" have sent spooky shivers down many an appreciative spine.

The real standout track, however – greeted from the opening drum riff by celebratory cheers – is Bela Lugosi's Dead. On this classy, atmospheric tribute to Hollywood's greatest Dracula, originally released as Bauhaus's first single, looped guitar effects and tentative pattering drums build up the tension before the booming four-note bassline breaks in like the tolling of a bell. Murphy stalks around in full-on bat mode, leering at the audience and intoning his campily dark lyrics, before giving way to a distinctly trippy, psychedelic guitar solo.

The album's other highlight, less satisfying musically perhaps, yet undeniably more of an "event", is the guest appearance of Nico – honorary member of the undead – on the closing Waiting For The Man. She blithely repays the deference she's given by her onstage companions by ignoring them altogether, eschewing such petty considerations as getting the words, let alone the timing, right. As the band chugs bravely on, chord changes are mistimed and misplaced, lyrics forgotten, and sections omitted, in a marvellous, unforgettably unskilled stab at a notoriously simple piece of music. Shambolic and wonderful.

Bauhaus's jerky, whiter-than-white dance reputation was founded on the extra twist of anxiety added by Ash's drenching, shredded guitar to the driving energy of punk, as showcased on stomping tracks like Kick In The Eye, In Fear Of Fear, and Dancing. Murphy's full melodramatic potential is best expressed on Dark Entries, with its distinct Velvet-Underground groove, or through the caged menace of Hair Of The Dog. Too self-aware to lapse into mere pomposity, but nonetheless capable of sincere and moving performance, Bauhaus were a stunning live act who took Goth-rock to its high-water mark.

➲ We almost chose **Mask**, Beggars Banquet, 1981

# Beach Boys

## Pet Sounds

Capitol, 1966

Brian Wilson (gtr, kbds, vocals), Bruce Johnston (vocals), Mike Love (vocals), Terry Melcher (vocals), Carl Wilson (vocals), Dennis Wilson (vocals), Alan Jardine (vocals), Carol Kaye (bass), Hal Blaine (drums).

Still the ultimate "studio album", **Pet Sounds** is the careful, mature, and all but perfect expression of the hopes and beliefs of a troubled young artist. Only 23 when he began work on the project, Brian Wilson had during the previous four hectic years developed a fascination with recording technology and techniques. Despite the Beach Boys' carefully cultivated image, he had never been the surfin', hot-roddin' type, and, by 1966, after sixteen top-forty singles and eleven albums of brainless summer, he'd said enough on the subject. Now, with the band away on tour without him, he and collaborator Tony Asher embarked upon crafting lyrics of introspection and melancholy, and then placing them reverentially on velvet cushions of melody. Just in time for the psychedelic mayhem of the late Sixties, Pet Sounds directed rock music towards the wide palette of sounds that could be achieved through dedicated studio time.

The pressures of keeping the Beach Boys in the charts, while coping with his own personal troubles and the temptations offered by success, had led Brian towards obsession and paranoia. Seeing Phil Spector as a rival had spurred him to match and surpass Spector in studio wizardry. Now the double challenge presented by the songs of Bob Dylan and the musical innovations of the *Rubber Soul*-era Beatles unleashed a flood of complex emotions, expressed in bewildering songs with baffling arrangements. This drug-fuelled search for perfection was shockingly confessional for the time, and was initially treated with disdain not only by much of the Beach Boys' audience, but even within the band itself (Mike Love dismissed it as "Brian's ego music").

During endless experiments, Wilson used his fellow Beach Boys as empty vessels, mere instruments to generate the requisite cut-glass harmonies, as he constructed shimmering walls of music that owed both inspiration and a percentage of the personnel to Phil Spector. From the young-love yearnings of the opener, Wouldn't It Be Nice, to the sadness of love gone wrong on the final cut, we follow a painful path of illicit romance, as innocence is lost through gentle lust and misplaced trust, all delicately coloured with sweeping strings and hints of woodwind.

Amid the technical details, it's easy to lose sight of the tender emotion in both the music and the deft precision of the lyrics. Witness the ornate beauty of the instrumental Let's Go Away For A While, or the understated sincerity of the words to God Only Knows – surely the love song they use in Heaven.

Despite the soul-searching of You Still Believe In Me and That's Not Me, and the hints of regret in Don't Talk (Put Your Head On My Shoulder and I'm Waiting For The Day, the songs are never maudlin, buoyed up by expressive dynamics and rich, inventive texturing. That said, of course, Sloop John B, a fan-pleasing singalong with a stunning acappella hook, has all the delicacy and tenderness of "Louie, Louie".

I Just Wasn't Made For These Times is a meditation on life as a misunderstood artist, while the bemusing collage of Pet Sounds can be interpreted as a sound-picture of Wilson's general incomprehension. The closing track, Caroline No, revisits the album's major themes, and seems to herald Wilson's imminent retreat into his reclusive – some might say ongoing – "sandbox" period, when his daring, focused exploration of the potential of the recording studio came to be replaced by directionless doodling. Far from the beach party, it was all ending in tears.

⟳ We almost chose **Wild Honey**, Capitol, 1968

# The Beatles

## Revolver

Parlophone, 1966

John Lennon (gtr, vocals), Paul McCartney (bass, vocals), George Harrison (gtr, vocals), Ringo Starr (drums, vocals).

From the opening amplifier hum, clearing of the throat and count-in, to the final tape collage with which it closes, **Revolver** is a studio album par excellence. John, Paul, and producer George Martin can be heard at the peak of their mutual comprehension, treating the studio as just another new instrument to be played, and the experimentation, kept in check by Martin's professionalism, works without becoming overwhelming. Building on the great leap forward of *Rubber Soul* and continuing their progression away from pop music towards psychedelic rock and Dylan-inspired "statements", the band stuck to their determination not to tour and released only one single (Eleanor Rigby/Yellow Submarine) from the album. *Revolver*'s delicate balance of straightforward tunes and acid whimsy leaves no unpleasant aftertaste, unlike the overblown *Sgt Pepper* (1967), which went on to outsell it, and is, both lyrically and musically, a superior project.

Glowing with bright new ideas, *Revolver* shows the Beatles responding to perceived threats from the US musical brigade, and coming out with all guns blazing. Essentially a McCartney solo, "Eleanor Rigby" crossed over to mainstream "adult" radio in spite of the enigmatic lyrics, thanks largely to its deft arrangement. The sitar and tablas make their first appearance in mainstream rock in Love You To, where George's "lost in the mystic" vocals are still in touch with his earthly desires, hoping to "make love all day long, make love singing songs". Even "Yellow Submarine" brought in taped effects of sea sounds, bells and whistles, biscuit-tin drums, well-structured vocal harmonies, and yet more brass band effects, to give everyone a lift.

The lighter-weight tracks on *Revolver* can be taken as innocent trills, celebrating good times; their magic emerges from reading between the lines. On Good Day Sunshine, for example, McCartney is having lots more fun than he should. The words are ambiguous enough to pass as just another love song, but there's a rollicking, honky-tonk jolliness that love alone can't explain. The jolly feel continues on Lennon's And Your Bird Can Sing, a dipping of the toe into the sea of anti-materialism, with its Byrds-style shimmering guitar line. Even Taxman, a Harrison composition, opens with a kicking riff, and the power behind George's blistering guitar breaks cannot be denied. Lennon returned to the microphone to sneer on She Said, She Said, famously inspired by Peter Fonda's lengthy tale one night of a surgical operation which almost went horribly wrong. Complex rhythms underpin the conversational lyrics in a glimpse of the darkside, as seen through Lennon's eyes.

The album closes with two extremely powerful tracks, coming from completely different musical directions. On Got To Get You Into My Life, we have the Beatles' take on soul music, with a Memphis-Horns-styled brass section backing McCartney as he screams and strains his way through the words in a fair stab at Otis Redding. For Tomorrow Never Knows, by contrast, we get the full blast of Lennon's inner psyche, with drones, guitars played backwards, dreadfully complicated drum patterns from Ringo, sped-up or slowed-down tapes, and lyrics of the purest, unblemished mystic drivel.

While *Revolver* was certainly informed by the drug experience – just look at the "sunglasses worn indoors" photos, and the artwork by old Hamburg pal Klaus Voormann, let alone the lyrics – it was recorded during a period of moderation and experiment, before it had all become just another boring habit, and is a better album as a result.

➲ We almost chose **Sgt Pepper's . . .**, Parlophone, 1967

# Beck

## Odelay

Geffen, 1996

Beck (vocals, organ, gtr, bass, harmonica, pcn, celeste, drums, kbds, pno, clavinet, slide gtr), Mike Boito (organ, trumpet), David Brown (sax), Charlie Haden (bass), Greg Leisz (pedal steel gtr), Mike Millius (screams), Joey Waronker (pcn, drums).

What made Beck one of the more compelling artists of the Nineties was the fact that, unlike just about all his contemporaries, he wasn't afraid of making an ass out of himself. At a time when the vast majority of pop musicians were hiding behind their samplers, Beck was always willing to take a risk. While his hipster compatriots trawled the thrift stores and exchanged knowing glances over the kitsch of obsolete pop culture, Beck harnessed hip-hop's beat archeology to a bid to form the detritus of the past into a coherent culture – one that might be able to embrace something other than an ironic distance.

That's not to say that **Odelay** isn't ironic or funny, just that it has something else going for it as well. It's the album that every media-literate child of the Eighties could have made, but didn't. A generation's worth of half-remembered catchphrases, references, hand-me-downs, readymades and information overload cohered like a Kurt Schwitters' collage, and thereby introduced a genuinely new identity into this world of constant flux. A lot of the credit for its success must go to producers the Dust Brothers (also architects of that other great admixture of media left-overs, the Beastie Boys' *Paul's Boutique*). The cut'n'paste aesthetic of hip-hop which they brought to the party mingled perfectly with Beck's own disembodied soundbite songwriting.

Trying to make sense of rootless post-Sixties youth culture, Beck pilfered poses and sounds from the sacred cows of American rock radio, and injected them with the ennui of a generation which had been told time and again that it would never change the world like its predecessors. Filled with lyrical gems like "Don't call us when the new age gets old enough to drink", and "Invite me to the Seventies", **Lord Only Knows** is Beck's pastiche of the Rolling Stones' world-weary *Sticky Fingers* booze-blues. **Jack Ass** sounds like a Scott McKenzie who's forgotten to wear flowers in his hair, while choruses elsewhere hark back to the decadent country-rock hoedowns of the Eagles. Beck may be ambivalent about "classic rock", but he never forsakes its virtues. Perhaps paradoxically, by combining hip-hop's "two turntables and a microphone" approach with the self-awareness of neo-folk, he rocks as hard as anyone of his time.

Like other children of the information age, Beck and the Dust Brothers took *Odelay* well beyond the traditional confines of rock and folk. **Derelict** is Tom Waits re-interpreted by a Balinese gamelan orchestra with some help from psychedelic hip-hoppers New Kingdom, while you'd swear that's Sly Stone's calliope whirling in the background of **Sissyneck**. Throughout that track, the sub-bass and drum machines of Eighties hip-hop explode out of the mix; the clavinets, drum breaks and funny voices of Seventies soul drop punchlines like Rudy Ray Moore; and the misguided futurism of sampled Moog maestro Dick Hyman reminds you of a time when technology was funny and charming and didn't pose a threat to your job.

Fusing a Bontempi organ riff with handclaps, Blue Note horn charts, a Mantronix snippet heard from a passing boom-box, and lines like "passing the dutchie from coast to coast", **Where It's At** is the climax of the whole patchwork assemblage. Remaking songs like "House of Blue Lights", "Sam's Place" and "Funky Broadway" for po-faced hipsters who'd forgotten how to dance, it accomplished everything pop music was always supposed to do, but, in the Nineties, so rarely did.

➲ We almost chose **Mutations**, Geffen, 1998

# Chuck Berry

## The Great Twenty-Eight

Chess, 1984

Chuck Berry (gtr, vocals), other musicians include Johnny Johnson (pno), Jasper Thomas (drums).

Without any exaggeration, this book would not exist without Chuck Berry. Something called rock'n'roll would have happened with or without the songs collected on **The Great Twenty-Eight** – rock'n'roll was already gathering momentum when Maybellene hit the airwaves in 1955 – but it wouldn't have the same swing, the same force, the same meaning. Berry was rock'n'roll's greatest songwriter, greatest performer, and greatest guitarist. Without him, there would be no Rolling Stones, no Beatles, no Beach Boys, no Bob Dylan, no MC5, no New York Dolls, no Aerosmith, no Slade, no Pretenders, no Oasis. Basically, if Chuck Berry hadn't come along, rock'n'roll might be nothing more than Elvis singing "Clambake" and "Ain't No Room to Rhumba in a Sports Car".

The irony that the greatest commentator of America's economic golden age was an African-American, and thus largely excluded from the postwar spoils, was far from lost on Berry himself. His records were riddled with contradictions, and on the best of them that ambivalence was close to the surface. As you'd expect from a dreamer, however, Berry's songs transcended their origins by aspiring to, and attaining, the power of myth.

Rock'n'roll has no more resonant myth than that of Johnny B. Goode. While the tale of "a country boy . . . who never, ever learned to read or write so well / But he could play the guitar just like ringing a bell" – Berry originally wrote "a coloured boy", but that would never be played on the radio – is the stuff of dreams, the real source of its earth-shattering force was the greatest guitar riff in the history of recorded music. In a few quick-fire notes, the "Johnny B. Goode" riff crystallized the essence of rock'n'roll: flash, urgency, overdrive, breathlessness, heat. With the exception of James Brown's "Cold Sweat" and the Sex Pistols' "Anarchy in the UK", no record has ever leapt out from the grooves the way "Johnny B. Goode" did.

That said, Berry's first single, "Maybellene" – based on the country standard "Ida Red" – came close. As a black artist interpreting "white" material, Berry was reversing the Elvis formula; he showed that Sam Phillips' dictum about finding a white man who could sing like a Negro was more than just exploitation, it was actually an equation that said something fundamental about America. Then again, no country singer ever sang lines like "As I was motorvatin' over the hill" or "Rain water blowin' all under my hood / I knew that it was doin' my motor good"; or ever admitted that the woman had the faster car; or had a drummer like Jasper Thomas banging furiously in the background.

For all Thomas's epic stomp, Berry's longtime pianist Johnny Johnson is one of the great unsung heroes of rock'n'roll. As demonstrated on You Can't Catch Me and Let it Rock, many of Berry's guitar figures were based on Johnson's barrelhouse licks, which grounded his sound in the very blues tradition that his guitar and lyrics were rendering a thing of the past.

While he was consigning the blues to history, Berry was creating the sound of the future. Roll Over Beethoven, perhaps the most arrogant record ever made, remains rock's most effective manifesto. Brown Eyed Handsome Man said it loud that Berry was black and proud, while every glam-rock song ever stole its guitar riff from Little Queenie. All that stops *The Great Twenty-Eight* from being the ultimate rock'n'roll album is that it fails to include his two best post-prison songs, "Promised Land" and "You Never Can Tell".

⮑ We almost chose **The Chess Box**, Chess, 1998

# Big Brother & The Holding Company

## Cheap Thrills

Columbia, 1968

Janis Joplin (vocals), Sam Andrew (gtr, bass), James Gurley (gtr), Peter Albin (bass), Dave Getz (drums).

Big Brother and the Holding Company were a band before Janis Joplin ever joined them. When Chet Helms, godfather to the mid-Sixties musical scene in San Francisco, suggested the link-up in 1966, several members were initially reluctant to let the singer come on board. Without her input, however, they'd have been written off as just another interestingly named psychedelic group. As for Joplin herself, she gained more than simply a springboard for her immense voice; she gained consistency. **Cheap Thrills**, their debut album for Columbia, has a continuity and coherence missing from the many posthumous compilations, showcasing Janis with the soulful sweetness and iron of Aretha Franklin or James Brown. Despite its troubled creation, it boasts her most assured and powerful performances, capturing into the bargain the California psychedelic scene just as it exploded onto the world stage.

By the time *Cheap Thrills* was released, the Big-Brother brand of shouting rock'n'roll and brooding blues had torn the Monterey Pop Festival of 1967 apart, and further touring had built up a huge sense of anticipation. The album itself was originally planned as a totally live document, but sections had to be re-recorded in the studio when it became clear they hadn't made enough recordings of sufficient quality on the road. Those studio sessions in turn were so chaotic, ripped apart by fights and ego clashes, that producer John Simon washed his hands of the project and had his name removed from the sleeve credits. All the more amazing, then, that *Cheap Thrills* worked so well, sold so well, and still ranks as one of the great early-psychedelic recordings, messy in parts but full of good intentions.

Acid-rock freakouts became commonplace so quickly that it's easy to sneer at the now-cliched distortion'n'feedback frenzy with which the album opens, let alone the occasional frankly loopy blizzard of notes later on. Taken in context, however, these were revolutionary musical developments that went on to influence rock music for the next ten years.

Though self-evidently a star in her own right, Janis takes backing vocals on two of the seven tracks, making room for Sam Andrews' quirky, folk-tinged rock'n'roll voice. Even in these cases, however, her distinctive, bluesy wail cuts through. With slick guitar work, feisty drumming, and intelligently structured bass, the band all pull their weight, but it's obvious, from the moment Joplin starts to sing, that she's the prime asset. Holding back during the first part of Combination Of The Two, she steps away from the mike mid-way through to unleash her belting, whisky-gravel voice, easily matching the guitar-fed-through-a-jet-engine pyrotechnics at the front of the stage. She remains further back during Oh Sweet Mary, contributing to the slower, catch-your-breath sections which punctuate the jazzier, guitar-led heroics that make up the bulk of its substance.

*Cheap Thrills* only truly begins to glow, however, when Joplin takes lead vocal. From the blues-stripped-bare of Turtle Blues, a Joplin composition that sounds exactly like Bessie Smith, to the shambling, heart-rending tragedy of Ball And Chain, where Joplin wanders off the beat during the first chorus in a sweeping, conversational, at-times screaming journey through whispers of love and cries of pain, it shines with a breathtaking beauty. Piece Of My Heart and Summertime, the standout tracks, boast huge, strong, booming vocals, delicate psychedelic guitar and howls of feedback angst that remain stunning thirty years later.

➲ We almost chose **Janis**, Columbia, 1993

# Bikini Kill

## The CD Version Of The First 2 Records

Kill Rock Stars, 1994

Kathleen Hanna (vocals), Tobi Vail (drums), Billy Karren (guitar), Kathi Wilcox (bass).

THE C.D. VERSION OF THE FIRST TWO RECORDS.

Above all other considerations, **The CD Version . . .** is a great punk rock album, angry from beginning to end, which addresses a range of serious issues – from incest and rape, through lesbian politics, to questioning the role of women in western society. Punk rock didn't go away when it stopped attracting headlines in the mainstream press, and the music business diverted the kids towards New Romance or the revival of mod. It just went underground, whence it continued to bubble periodically to the surface, like lava with bad attitude.

Bikini Kill first emerged in Olympia, the capital of Washington state in the far northwestern US, in 1991, when an early version of Feels Blind was included on the *Kill Rock Stars* compilation album, and eclipsed an early Nirvana track in the process. Subsequently re-recorded, the track re-appeared, with five others, on the *Bikini Kill* mini-LP (also 1991). The remaining seven tracks here are drawn from the 1992 split album *Yeah Yeah Yeah Yeah*, which they shared with Huggy Bear, a London-based band with broadly similar, genuine girl-power aims.

Exploiting punk's traditional broad brush, and gift for turning the spoken word into song lyrics, the challenges begin in Double Dare Ya. This girl-on-girl provocation to stand up and break the conditioning comes replete with a chugging, rocking riff and explosions of noise, while the words swiftly splutter beyond English into a language of incandescent rage – "Double triple fucking dipple fucking dare ya . . . Girl-fucking-friend". In Liar, the broad brush becomes a spray gun, as the lyrics explore meat-eating, black-hating, wife-beating and rape, turning harrowing as Ono/Lennon's "Give Peace A Chance" refrain is drowned out by blood-freezing screams. Carnival – the album's outstanding mosh-pit favourite – opens with "this is a song about sixteen-year-old girls giving head to carnies for free rides and hits of pot"; you can't get much plainer speaking than that.

The version of "Feels Blind" here is even more powerful than that which stood out on the *KRS* compilation. Slow burning at the start, an oblique and distinctive tale of numbness and isolation, it's the most thought-provoking track on the album. Thurston Hearts The Who, which follows, blends a voice reading magazine articles about the band with another which is following the lyric sheet – an "art punk" moment worthy of Patti Smith's more inventive earlier works.

Though the songs drip with outrage and venom, they're far more than mere humourless diatribes. In Suck My Left One, another powerblast of guitars and drums, incest and parental denial are dealt a heavy dose of verbal slapstick, while Rebel Girl is a knowing re-write of the "Leader Of The Pack" stereotype – all sleazy, rock'n'roll hero-worship. Even White Boy – which blazes anger – starts off by giving a dumb guy the chance to make a total fool of himself, expressing his opinions on tape.

Both in the US and overseas, Bikini Kill are persistently lumped together with other all-female acts as part of a "riot grrrl" scene, a lazy label that amounts to little more than a convenient way to pigeonhole diverse female artists despite widely differing agendas. Before the band finally fizzled out in 1998, they always insisted that their music deserved to be assessed on its own merits, and refused attempts by journalists to tag them as leaders of any movement. Fiercely loyal to the underground, with sleevenotes as painfully typed and utterly sincere as a revolutionary manifesto, they gave a new voice to punk rock, while carrying the flame forward for a few more years.

➲ We almost chose **Pussy Whipped**, Kill Rock Stars, 1993

# The Birthday Party

## Junkyard

4AD, 1982

Nick Cave (vocals), Rowland Howard (gtr, sax), Tracey Pew (bass), Barry Adamson (bass), Phil Calvert (drums), Mick Harvey (everything).

Arty, outstanding originators, the Birthday Party were responsible for some of the strangest and most compelling noises in rock history. A nightmarish cross between Joy Division and Captain Beefheart, they brought a macabre humour and ferocious dark intelligence to the post-punk scene. With Cave, the new-wave Byron, booming lyrics of disaster and screaming sounds of torment, they were chaotic, scary and very, very loud.

**Junkyard**, the third Birthday Party album, was recorded in London, where, in exile from their native Melbourne, Australia, the band had built up a fanatically devoted audience. Utterly at odds with the work of their contemporaries, and unlike anything that has come since, their music is hard to classify. It's certainly uncompromising, even demanding, but it's also exciting, passionate and dangerous, and it went on to influence much of the mid-Eighties industrial scene. Ripe with the classic early-Goth fascination with the grotesque, they were also prime movers in the Goth movement. Individual band members later worked with such varied acts as Psychedelic Furs, Einstürzende Neubaten, and Lydia Lunch, as well, of course, as Nick Cave and the Bad Seeds.

From the blazing heat of Blast Off! – similar in feel to Pere Ubu's Cleveland thrash – the Birthday Party rage full-on throughout the album. There's a touch of Public Image-era John Lydon here, a blast of no-wave noise guitar there, clamouring for attention against a backdrop of modulated shrieks and sound effects. The Dim Locator is a sustained rant of freshly minted words that claws frantically at your sleeve, while Several Sins re-writes the "Fever" riff with twangy, swampy guitars, and shares a sweaty bed of shame with Kewpie Doll. On She's Hit, Cave veers between yelps of pain and a crooning delight in violence, but things are nowhere darker than on Kiss Me Black, where his grunted vocals only briefly break into comprehensibility, rhyming "stink on us", "incubus", "succubus" and "fuck to us", as the song lurches from fast to stop and back again.

While the broad-brush cartoon-style lyrics feature some devastating pen-portraits, a large part of the allure of the songs stems from their fragmentary approach. Stories often remain half told, glimpsed in almost unintelligible vignettes. Dead Joe, for example, borrows from J G Ballard in its depiction of a traffic accident as both sculpture and junk, rather than simply the setting for Joe's final moments. Neither of the album's two versions even approaches logical narrative. Similarly, Hamlet (Pow, Pow, Pow) is a witches' brew of intricate drumming, with a lyrical nod towards Patti Smith's version of "Gloria". Shakespeare quotes blend with gangster-movie imagery, with Cave providing the punctuation by shouting "Pow!" into the mike at maximum volume.

The real showstoppers of the set are Big Jesus Trash Can – in which Cave's demented shouting battles hand-to-hand with the output of the rhythm section, all refereed by Mick Harvey's crazy sax – and the title track, Junkyard, a megalomanic epic of slow, carefully paced growling vocals and frenetic repetition. The final curtain falls after Release The Bats – full of scratchy, bitey, horror-sex delivered by a Nick on the far side of losing control.

Junkyard showcases the Birthday Party – a superb live band, with a huge following even today, more than fifteen years since they split up – at their absolute best. It's a feast of dramatic music, plump with extremes of tragedy and comedy, and jolting forward on the brink of collapse.

➲ We almost chose **Hits**, 4AD, 1992

# Björk

## Debut

One Little Indian, 1993

Björk (vocals, kbd, producer). Musicians include Garry Hughes (kbds), Corky Hale (orchestral harp), Marius De Vries (kbds), Talvin Singh (tabla), Luis Jardim (bass, pcn), Nellee Hooper (pcn, producer).

On **Debut**, her career-defining first solo release since leaving the poppier Sugarcubes, Björk achieved the double success of presenting a female take on the still-new dance/rock field, while showcasing the most powerful and original voice of the decade. At first, the sheer novelty of her Icelandic space-Cockney voice, and the fragile Norse-elf image that went with it, diverted attention from her emotional power and intensity, and the skill with which she delivered her lyrics. Despite the expert musical accompaniment and excellent production throughout, however, Björk's clever phrasing and cathartic vocalizing are precisely what make *Debut* a great album.

*Debut* starts with the intensely "studio" production of Human Behaviour, a brooding study of the impossibility of getting along with other people, on which Nellee Hooper (producer for Massive Attack and Soul II Soul among others) immediately makes his presence felt. Crying, which follows, features a jazz-tinged, keyboard-driven riff and deceptively naive lyrics. Lapses from standard English ("Here everyone are so vulnerable and I'm as well") serve to emphasize the overall sense of vulnerability.

The gloom begins to lift in Venus As A Boy, with its gentle but distinctly percussive feel, and sex-drenched phrases like "his fingers focus on her". Any lingering hint of darkness is banished by the strobes and UV spotlights of There's More To Life Than This, with its good-vibes "live recording" feel and club-style loops. When Björk sneaks into the toilet for a line ("We could nick a little boat and sneak off to this island"), her precision London demotic and mischievous delivery come as a deliberate stand against faceless house music.

Next up, Corky Hale and her harp provide a carefully under-stated backing to Björk's respectful rendition of show tune Like Someone In Love. There's just enough to time to regain composure before she takes us back to the dancefloor with Big Time Sensuality – a love song to ecstasy and being in love. Released as a single, and a club hit in its many remixed versions, this was the track that crossed Björk over from the indie kids to the dance audience. A well-known face on the London scene, she concocted a straightforward good-times dance tune, with arch references to pills ("It's coming up") and hedonism ("I don't know my future after this weekend and I don't want to"), that celebrates summer in clubland.

The far gentler One Day, swathed in positivity over a slow house beat and given brassy touches by some delicate keyboard work, leads into Aeroplane, a sensitive study of regret and the loneliness that comes of forced separation. A complex saxophone intro, basking on a jazzy background of birdsong and bongos, gradually develops a sweltering, Latin feel as Björk pulls out all her vocal skills and lyrical passion. Björk's superb vocalizing comes into its own again on Come To Me, with its siren-like temptations and movie-music atmosphere, but even that is soon overshadowed by Violently Happy.

Anchor Song, yet another vocal showcase, features some strongly provocative imagery plus a difficult, attention-demand-ing saxophone break, before it leads into the harrowing Play Dead. Released as a single and featured in the movie soundtrack of *The Young Americans*, this final track displays vocal dynamics to match the pain in the lyrics ("I play dead and the hurting stops"), and brings *Debut* to a haunting, shuddering close.

➲ We almost chose **Post**, One Little Indian, 1995

# Black Sabbath

## Black Sabbath – Volume IV

Warner, 1972

Ozzy Osbourne (vocals), Tony Iommi (gtr), Geezer Butler (bass), Bill Ward (drums).

Many have tried to re-create the epic slabs of sound that were the very essence of Black Sabbath; none has succeeded. Having invented heavy metal and all its nasty offshoots (death, speed, you name it), as well as kickstarted grunge, and endured years of being critically reviled, the Sabs are now hailed as an influence on the likes of Ministry, Metallica, Nirvana and Marilyn Manson. Hell, even alternative country maestros Wilco have been known to play a Sabbath medley. Thirty years on, Black Sabbath still headline major festivals around the world – the "Ozzfests" – solely dedicated to the Sabbath school of headbanging.

The classic line-up of Black Sabbath – named after a Boris Karloff movie – that burst out of Birmingham in 1969 was fronted by Ozzy Osbourne, cartoon wildman extraordinaire. Who else could turn up on both the *South Park* album and Rick Wakeman's *Return To The Centre Of The Earth* within a matter of weeks? Guitarist Tony Iommi had previously stinted with Jethro Tull, but found that his true forte was in creating the monster riffs, underpinned by bassist Geezer Butler, that defined Black Sabbath and produced a maelstrom of distortion. The jazz inflections of under-rated drummer Bill Ward, however, were responsible for giving the music such a nimble edge.

Of Sabbath's early albums, 1972's **Volume IV** has to be the best, not least because it avoids the sagas of fairies (albeit with boots) and wizards with which Sabbath came to be associated. Ozzy's tongue has seldom strayed far from his cheek (except when he's biting the heads off bats), but the joke could wear thin after a while. In addition, *Volume IV* boasts some of Iommi's most gut-churning riffs, as well as some particularly deft instrumental passages.

The opener Wheels of Confusion, for instance, transforms from crunching power chords into a glorious Sergio Leone pastiche, overlaid with rippling guitars. Elsewhere, Supernaut starts out as a highland reel, but Ward's manic drumming soon kicks into Latin overdrive, and it ends up as an infectious slice of salsa. Laguna Sunrise, a beautiful Spanish guitar instrumental, is one of two quieter pieces that ease the album's otherwise relentless pace; the other, Changes, a ballad built around a simple piano motif, remains one of Sabbath's most affecting songs.

"When I think about those records, I remember the time we had when we were making them. That's why I like *Volume IV*," Ozzy told Q magazine. "We'd got the rock star fever by then – limousines everywhere, groupies, dealers dropping by with bags of white powder." The coke abuse, as detailed on Snowblind, had clearly got out of hand, as had the massive drinking bouts. *Volume IV* was written and rehearsed in a mansion in Bel Air, and in many ways the sheer hedonism of the whole process marked the beginning of the end for the original band. Ozzy got fat ("Sabs Fight The Flab" ran one memorable headline), while Iommi was bitten by the synth bug and drenched the next few albums in ersatz strings. The band reached an all-time sartorial low on the cover of *Sabotage*, which featured Ward wearing his wife's tights while Ozzy sported a kimono with platform boots.

By 1978, Ozzy had departed in acrimony to pursue what turned out to be a hugely successful solo career, leaving the others to plod on with a series of increasingly unsuccessful substitute vocalists. The inevitable reunion in 1998, after years of ill-health and backbiting, was loud, proud and lucrative. Inane? Yes. Plodding? Yes. Ridiculous? Yes. Magnificent? Yes!

➲ We almost chose **Paranoid**, Warner, 1974 / Castle 1996

# David Bowie

## The Rise and Fall of Ziggy Stardust and the Spiders from Mars

RCA, 1972

David Bowie (gtr, kbds, sax, vocals), Mick Ronson (gtr, pno, vocals), Trevor Bolder (bass), Mick "Woody" Woodmansey (drums), Rick Wakeman (kbds).

By opening the door for a million freaks and uptight kinks, **Ziggy Stardust** was the record that made David Bowie a worldwide star. Glam rock's first and best stab at the concept album, it loosely chronicles the rise of a rock'n'roll band to stardom, the deification of the group's mainman, and his subsequent descent, by way of arrogance and mental torment, into suicide. The snapshot imagery through which Bowie transmuted this tired old B-movie scenario into a rock album, and his ingenuity in setting it against the novel backdrop of a dying civilization, give it the urgency and vitality of a call to arms.

Which, in many ways, it was. In 1972, rock'n'roll – which had grown up hot, horny but definitely heterosexual – was no place for guys who dyed their hair carrot-orange, sported make-up offstage, or wore flimsy shirts, long enough to be dresses ("men's dresses", Bowie insisted in interviews). Borrowing heavily from the New York Dolls and Iggy Pop school of media management through outrage, Bowie reinvented himself as a polysexual rocker from another planet, coming out to the press first as gay, and then as bisexual, and turning taboo into a marketing tool.

The relatively sparse musical backing allows Bowie's voice plenty of space to roam and stomp around. On gentle acoustic shuffles like Soul Love and Starman, he's left free to muse on the many kinds of love, and the life-enhancing properties of a new music that your parents will never understand. However, it's not all swooning and hand-holding; Moonage Daydream is stuffed with predatory sexual imagery, while his "rock'n'rolling bitch" oozes lust from every seam in Come On. Similarly, Suffragette City, originally offered to Mott The Hoople, jumps right on your lap and wriggles.

Most of the second half of the album is taken up by songs that deal more explicitly with the Ziggy Stardust story, though they also deal with a world in decline and the simultaneous birth of a rock band. By this stage of his career, Bowie was exuberantly blurring the boundaries between his onstage characters and his offstage behaviour. Like Ziggy, he believed that to achieve stardom in the shortest possible time, it was necessary to act like a star. This blend of real life with fiction kept the album, concert tour, and indeed the whole concept safely clear of pomposity and arch self-parody; Ziggy believed in Ziggy, Bowie believed in Ziggy, and the fans couldn't help but follow suit.

In the sad tale of Lady Stardust, tinged with unrequited love, an early fan describes how Ziggy was discovered and whisked off into the stratosphere. Star, which follows, is a straight-ahead rock'n'roll fantasy that draws heavily on the Velvet Underground songbook. With Come On panting over the pre-AIDS pleasures of free love, Ziggy and the Spiders reach their peak. Then, in the torch song Lady Stardust, it all turns sour. As Ziggy starts to believe his own publicity, the band bitch backstage like a beer-fuelled Greek chorus. By the time Suffragette City is over, the kids have killed the man and the band has broken up. All that remains is the bedsit anthem Rock'n'Roll Suicide, badly strummed in countless lonely rooms.

For all its melodrama, and the odd lapse into patent daftness, the sincerity of Ziggy's requiem cannot be denied. With descendants as diverse as Marc Almond and Radiohead, Bowie's most fully realised concept album still stands as a proud achievement.

➲ We almost chose **Station to Station**, RCA, 1976

# James Brown

## Star Time

Polygram, 1991

James Brown (pno, drums, vocals, rap), plus a host of musicians.

James Brown has always understood what made pop music great in the first place: an immediacy and momentum that steamrollers any obstacles in its path. Brown is at once the most superficial musician in history, and the most profound: there is nothing below the surface of any of his performances, yet his links to a tradition a millennium old are glaringly obvious. Even if his actual recordings had never amounted to more than second-rate soul, Brown would be the Godfather for the simple reason that whether he was sporting his process or rocking the two-foot Afro, Brown was the most assertively *black* personality ever to be accorded mainstream acceptance in America. Like the other towering figures of American music – Louis Armstrong, Robert Johnson, and Ray Charles – it would be impossible to overstate his importance.

**Star Time** traces Brown's rise from his days as a sidewalk dancer in his hometown of Augusta, Georgia, to his status as the only musician who can match Elvis as an iconic presence. Brown and his Famous Flames exploded onto the music scene in 1956, with one of the most idiosyncratic singles ever, Please, Please, Please. Before re-writing every rule about the role of rhythm in western music, Mr Please Please laid waste to the standard notion of a ballad singer – a feat perhaps even more important. Ray Charles may have introduced the sound of gospel into r'n'b, but Brown brought the speaking-in-tongues possession of shouters like Archie Brownlee of the Five Blind Boys of Mississippi, and Claude Jeter of the Swan Silvertones, into popular music.

Beginning with his 1964 single, Out of Sight, and continuing through such landmarks as Papa's Got a Brand New Bag, I Got You (I Feel Good), Money Won't Change You, Let Yourself Go, Cold Sweat, There Was a Time, Ain't It Funky Now, Say It Loud – I'm Black and I'm Proud, and Funky Drummer, James Brown orchestrated a tectonic shift in the foundation of music. In a manner not far removed from the compositional methods of jazz artists like Charles Mingus or Duke Ellington, he'd sing and hum the drum-like guitar lines, the hard-bop horn charts and rhythm patterns, and the walking double-jointed basslines that begat funk, disco, hip-hop, house, techno and jungle to band leaders Nat Jones and Pee Wee Ellis, who then transcribed them for the other band members.

With 1970's Get Up (I Feel Like Being A) Sex Machine, Brown re-invented music once again. Only two things mattered about the record: Bootsy Collins' bass, which had more popping, slithering, sliding, strutting gangster lean than a hustlers' convention on Lennox Avenue, and his brother Catfish's tersely angular chicken-scratching on guitar. With almost nothing but Jabo Starks' drums for company, the liquid bass and rawboned guitar built up a staggering tension that ushered in the minimal militancy of the funk era.

More sparse funk mantras were to follow, before "The Original Disco Man" was eclipsed by a genre that took the concept of "Sex Machine" far more literally even than the man who invented it. While disco was streamlining the JB groove, its evil twin, hip-hop, celebrated the Godfather in all his polyrhythmic glory. It's safe to say that hip-hop would not exist without the "give the drummer some" interludes which James Brown injected into his records, and this might be James Brown's ultimate legacy. Groups like the Beatles and the Rolling Stones have inspired thousands of copyists, but only Brown has instigated several entire genres.

➲ We almost chose **Live At The Apollo Vol 1**, Polydor, 1963

# Jeff Buckley

## Grace

Columbia, 1995

Jeff Buckley (gtr, kbds, harp, vocals), Karl Berger (strings), Matt Johnson (pcn), Gary Lucas (gtr), Loris Holland (organ), Mick Grondahl (bass), Misha Masud (tabla), Michael Tighe (gtr).

Having burst from the comparative obscurity of the New York club scene to win an adoring worldwide audience with **Grace**, Jeff Buckley fell in with bad company (stumbling out of nightclubs alongside Courtney Love, for example), then drowned before he could complete his second full-length recording. He remains far more, however, than just another tragic rock casualty. He set out to combine the prequisite sensitivity and delicacy of any major singer-songwriter with his own brutally honest, grunge-informed sensibility, and, crucially, he had the voice – one moment a cooing angel, the next a howling gale of betrayed anguish – to carry it off.

The stepping stone that introduced Buckley's hard-edged, lost romancer looks, awesome vocal range, and outstanding ear for arrangement, was 1994's *Live At Sin-E* EP, on which he extending Van Morrison's "The Way Young Lovers Do" to ten breathtaking minutes. On *Grace*, recorded for a major label a year later, he surrounded himself with musicians and producers of rare ability, and gave his unique, soulful singing the space in which to swoop, whisper, caress and wail.

Buckley was capable of raw whisky'n'cigarettes rock (Eternal Life, with its Jimmy Page-tribute guitar intro and Led Zeppelin riffing), Leonard Cohen-style balladry (Hallelujah, a powerful celebration of love and sex that's structured like a hymn, and performed with an air of understated reverence), and full-on chorister treble (Corpus Christi Carol). On the album's best songs, he ranges from roaring macho man-done-wrong, through ethereal brink-of-orgasm gasps and sighs, to celebratory chorus within a single piece.

The title track Grace, for example, showcases Buckley's deft arrangements as much as it does his voice, which moves between bashful courtier and yelling soul man. A bouncy, rollicking intro moves back as Buckley hints at love, then turns to wild waltztime as it carries the melody seamlessly from note to note. Lilac Wine, another standout, has Buckley at his androgynous-choirboy angelic best, recasting an old torch song as an anthem. Tugging at the heartstrings as shamelessly as "You'll Never Walk Alone", the song peaks as he cracks into a choked sob. Hammy to an extent, but effective nonetheless.

Last Goodbye opens with conversational, end-of-relationship lyrics pitched over shafts of slide guitar and Pink Floyd-style pastoral riffing. It builds slowly until Buckley finally loses control, matching Curtis Mayfield for range and total commitment. A similarly sanctified harmonium sound, coupled with bluesy guitar work, highlights Buckley's quasi-religious approach to sex amid the intense yearning of Lover You Should've Come Over. Over a crescendo of glorious Hammond organ and heavenly choristers, he finally takes the song over the brink with the climactic line "She's a tear that hangs inside my soul forever".

*Grace* was a defining moment in rock, a once-in-a-generation album marking the emergence of a fully formed artist who was every bit the equal of his absentee father, Tim. An *Astral Weeks* for the Nineties, the raw sincerity with which Jeff Buckley pulled together a new yet timeless music from his hugely diverse sources stunned the blasé music industry. Perhaps he was born to lose, just like his dad, but that he died a romantic troubadour's death does nothing to diminish the appalling anti-climax.

➲ We almost chose . . . **My Sweetheart The Drunk**, Columbia, 1998

## Buzzcocks

# Singles Going Steady

United Artists/Liberty, 1979

Pete Shelley (gtr, vocals), Steve Diggle (bass, gtr), Steve Garvey (bass), John Maher (drums).

The Buzzcocks were the bittersweet romantics of punk, with a view that encompassed the sweaty, embarrassing and painful aspects of love while remaining equally ready to celebrate its breathtaking, runaway excitement. One of Britain's earliest punk bands, formed in 1976 by Pete Shelley and singer Howard Devoto after seeing a Sex Pistols gig, the Buzzcocks started out as a standard-issue dour punk band, fronted by Devoto's intense snarl and Shelley's buzzsaw guitar, releasing the "Spiral Scratch" EP on their own label.

Following Devoto's unexpected departure to form Magazine in 1977, Shelley shifted to lead vocal and writing duties. Once bassist Garth was replaced by Steve Garvey, the band gelled. Swiftly signed to a major label, United Artists, they produced a string of the decade's most uplifting hit singles, and in the process returned style, glamour and street-smart flash to a punk scene that was already becoming excessively depressed and self-centred. The Buzzcocks were a band to fall in love with, for their vulnerability, their honesty, and above all the joy they brought with every latest record.

There was a change in lyrical focus too, as issue-based, "big picture" social realism was abandoned in favour of intimate, personal stories. Although they recorded three successful albums, including the masterful *Another Music In A Different Kitchen*

(1978), they were at their best confined to seven inches of vinyl and a four-minute maximum song length. **Singles Going Steady** collects the A- and B-sides of the eight singles they recorded during the golden years of 1978 and 1979, six of which made the UK charts.

The lasting appeal of the Buzzcocks stems equally from their sardonic wit, the cheeky one-string guitar solos, Shelley's perpetually misunderstood adolescent whine, and the irresistibly breathless pace of the whole ensemble. True to their punk roots, they were never afraid to say the occasional naughty word or to peek behind the bedroom door – witness the tongue-twisting verbal gymnastics of Orgasm Addict, their first single, backed by the speedy-yet-wistful ranting of Whatever Happened To?

During the stunning sequence of releases that ensued – What Do I Get?/Oh Shit (the first actual hit), I Don't Mind/Autonomy, Love You More/Noise Annoys, and Ever Fallen In Love/Just Lust, Shelley matured as a lyricist, his down-to-earth imagery drawing favourable comparisons with such elder statesmen of rock as Ray Davies of the Kinks. Later on, the band developed a neo-psychedelic feel, traceable through Promises/Lipstick, Everybody's Happy Nowadays/Why Can't I Touch It? – a mystic vision of the universal, not the hormone-driven grope anthem you might expect – and Harmony In My Head/Something's Gone Wrong Again. By now Diggle had been brought in as co-writer, and he's credited with total responsibility for "Harmony In My Head".

At their best, the Buzzcocks created a new kind of pop music: one that confronted the problems of the day in the language of the day, and thus made them small and personal enough to deal with. With ten of these sixteen tracks focusing on relationships, generally in some kind of trouble, the Buzzcocks can seem as superficially dismissive of love as Johnny Rotten – never more so than in "Oh Shit" or "Just Lust". What redeems them, however, is that all the songs look upwards and forwards, certain that there's better around the corner, somewhere ahead.

➲ We almost chose **Another Music In A Different Kitchen**, UA, 1978

# John Cale

## Fear

Island, 1974

John Cale (vocals, kbds, gtr, bass), Phil Manzanera (gtr), Charlie Leggatt (bass),
Fred Smith (drums), I. & D. Chanter and L. Strike (girls), Eno (Eno).

Multi-talented, classically-trained, associate of cutting-edge experimentalists and ex-member of the Velvet Underground, John Cale comes with an impressive pedigree. Both through his own recordings and through his collaborations with others, he's the quintessential grain of sand that seeds the pearl. Having moved to New York from his native Wales in order to study with minimalist masters such as La Monte Young and John Cage, Cale in turn became a musical *eminence grise*. In the decade after he left the Velvets, he helped to shape the nascent punk scenes in both the US and the UK, producing debut recordings by artists as diverse as the Stooges, the Modern Lovers, Patti Smith, Alternative TV and Squeeze.

Throughout that period and beyond, Cale also released a stream of cultured, intelligent albums that were nonetheless permeated with both the lightness of the best pop and the darkness of the Velvets at their peak. With **Fear** in particular, surrounded by a band of impeccable musicians, he shaped a collection of memorable pieces of the greatest subtlety and wit. Moving away from the hardcore minimalism he'd explored in the past, Cale turned instead to songcraft, creating, in *Fear*, a wide-ranging spread of moods and atmospheres, from luscious slices of idealized Americana to stark sounds of destruction and collapse. Two of the most intriguing and memorable songs on the album –

**Buffalo Ballet** and **Ship Of Fools** – portray charmingly bucolic episodes in the gradual maturing of the nation. Borrowing from the many streams of American folk music, Cale explores the voice itself, rather than the words it delivers, as the medium of communication; the unsophisticated lyrics signify little in comparison to the rich emotional content of his careful tones.

With a nod towards the ambient music of Brian Eno, **Emily**, a love song that swells and retreats like waves on a beach, also employs naive lyrics to convey deep emotion. **Fear Is A Man's Best Friend**, by contrast, is a deceptively chirpy piano-driven groove, with considered lyrics and a dumbly depressed chorus, that decays into one of Cale's characteristic keyboard-destroying rants. The humorous, bouncy feel and cheerful negativity are picked up in **Barracuda**, another poke at death that's jollied along by gorgeous guitar sounds and a smile-inducing fiddle solo. **You Know More Than I Know** takes a knowing, country-tinged peek, through the bottom of a glass, at the prospect of future pain and sorrow.

**Momamma Scuba** – the slide-guitar-drenched episode of lust and sweat with which the album closes – boasts yet more of Cale's trademark unstoppable riffs, but Cale is truly seen at his swaggering best on two other, widely diverse, standouts. **Gun** tells a tale of murder and blood, wrapped in a disjointed, piano-propelled boogie. Aided by an appropriately gloomy guitar break and some totally insane soloing, this horror story extends to eight minutes, without ever pausing to draw breath. **The Man Who Couldn't Afford To Orgy** turns its back on angst to embrace decadence and melancholy. Perversely pronouncing "orgy" with a hard "g", as in "gun", this sinister waltz is all frills, whispers, and dreamy female vocals, with the only soloing coming from a discreet, laid-back, mellow guitar.

*Fear* is the definitive statement by one of the most influential of rock musicians. Uncompromising and covering a stunning amount of territory, while always remaining accessible, it's the high point of all John Cale's solo guitar- and piano-based work.

➲ We almost chose **Fragments Of A Rainy Season**, Hannibal, 1992

# Can

## Tago Mago

Spoon, 1971

Irmin Schmidt (kbds, vocals), Holger Czukay (bass), Michael Karoli (gtr, violin), Jaki Leibezeit (drums), Kenji "Damo" Suzuki (vocals).

While psychedelic music often consists of little more than patchouli-reeking long-hairs playing their bongos in the mud and spouting acid-fried drivel, when it does live up to its name it's capable of altering perceptions and opening up panoramas of possibility. Perhaps paradoxically, psychedelia works best when it aims its reality distortions at the body as well as the head. No one was more successful at this fusion of mind and body than the kings of Krautrock, Can.

Former disciples of the godfather of electronic music, composer Karlheinz Stockhausen, Can were turned on to the possibilities of rock by the Velvet Underground. After two albums of garage rock that beat with the "motorik" pulse of industry rather than blues-based swing, they set up their own Inner Space studio inside a castle in Cologne. Ensconced in their medieval digs, they'd improvize for hours on end. The tapes of these jam sessions were then edited into something approaching coherent song form by bassist Holger Czukay, whereupon vocalist Damo Suzuki would scat, mumble, sing in Japanese, and rant over the top like a more mellow, more graceful Shaun Ryder.

The first fruits of this new methodology were found on 1971's sprawling double album, **Tago Mago**. Naming the album after a mythical magician, these sorcerers of sound escaped from the straitjacket of psychedelia, pulled a rabbit from a hat, and created some of the most tactile, most freakish and spaciest music this side of electric Miles Davis. Tempering their experimental instincts with catchy hooks, and riding a groove that somehow melded the Velvets with James Brown, Can not only fed your head, but they made it nod to the beat as well.

*Tago Mago* begins with a lustrous shimmer of guitar echo and synth squiggle reminiscent of early Jamaican dub. Like King Tubby and Lee Perry, Can explored how mixing-board technology could elasticate the boundaries of the "song" – a process they called "flow motion". While they never penetrated dub's caverns of bass, Can did traverse its world of echo, and their pioneering mixture of rock noise and attitude with funk's Brownian motion would later crop up in records by Public Image Limited, Talking Heads, Moonshake, Laika and Tortoise, to name a few.

The opening track, Paperhouse, showcases both Karoli's trebly, implausibly crystalline guitar sound and Leibezeit's debt to the great Stax drummer Al Jackson, Jr., before it mutates into a propulsive psych-out. Mushroom features a beat that shuffles like an agitated Clyde Stubblefield, while Oh Yeah was the kind of anthemic, lysergic mumbo-jumbo of which Syd Barrett always dreamed. These good-footed workouts culminate with the monster jam, Halleluhwah. Building on the tidal flow of Leibezeit's percussive waves and Czukay's bass pull, Karoli and Schmidt throw shapes everywhere and sculpt with a battery of effects pedals, while phantom violins and harpsichords heighten the sense of disorientation.

Sounding like the theme to a Fifties sci-fi B-movie that had its popcorn spiked, the 17-minute Aumgn marks where Stockhausen enters the mix. Inspired by his urge to create electronic mantras and to fuse all world music into an organic whole, "Aumgn" is a tape collage that attempts to make the Hindu notion of "Aum" (the sound that encompasses the entirety of the world) flesh. Both Peking O and the sitar-fuelled Bring Me Coffee or Tea play with similar ideas, bringing Krautrock's masterwork to a close by taking the world in a love embrace.

➲ We almost chose **Unlimited Edition**, Spoon/Mute, 1976

# Captain Beefheart and his Magic Band

## Trout Mask Replica

Reprise, 1969

Captain Beefheart (vocals, gtr, harp, clarinet, sax), Rockette Morton (bass, vocals), Zoot Horn Rollo (flute, gtr), Antennae Jimmy Semens (gtr), John French (drums), Jerry Handley (bass), Mascara Snake (clarinet, vocals), Douglas Moon (gtr), Frank Zappa (producer).

One shudders to imagine music lessons at the California high school which launched both Frank Zappa and Don Van Vliet (Captain Beefheart) into the world. When these two masters of the outer reaches of rock joined forces some years later, assembling in a rented house to create **Trout Mask Replica**, the scene must have been part studio, part outreach experiment for the criminally insane.

Despite its notoriously impenetrable, ear-threatening, free-jazz distractions, *Trout Mask Replica* is in many ways the ultimate blues album, conveying intense experiences under intense pressure. Beefheart's consummate musical triumph, it was the most explicit and complex avant-garde manifesto produced by the West-coast psychedelic movement of the Sixties, and its influence can be traced via Public Image all the way to Tortoise in the Nineties. A disturbing blend of total chaos with precisely charted, discordant music, it consistently out-weirds all contemporary and subsequent challenges, with Zappa's skills as producer displayed at their finest every time he decided to leave the tape running at the end of an apparently irretrievable take.

The 28 tracks are linked by "found" recordings, studio banter, and a number of obviously rehearsed acid-humour sketches.

These word games are echoed throughout the songs themselves, in which lyrics that often verge on gibberish are sprayed seemingly at random over the fractious guitar work of Jeff Cotton (renamed "Antennae Jimmy Semens" for the duration) and the percussion of John ("Drumbo") French.

On Moonlight On Vermont, an ultra-heavy riff later mimicked by King Crimson leads into a sketch about a squid eating dough in a polyethylene bag, probably the moment of purest madness in an album known for little else. At other points, Beefheart's music appears to have been salvaged, half-decayed, from earlier, more recognizable styles; Sweet, Sweet Bulbs, for example, resembles the laid-out remains of a long dead love song. As it segues into Neon Meate Dream Of A Octofish, the vocals themselves degenerate still further into a spitting, spasmodic stream of consciousness. China Pig, She's Too Much For My Mirror, and Well are the mutated descendants of the blues, while both Sugar'n'Spikes and Ant, Man, Bee must have started life as relatively normal rock songs.

Elsewhere, bursts of well-structured poetry are interspersed between islands of calm, neatly trimmed short stories (as in The Old Fart At Play, a surreal saga of wooden fish masks and geriatric love games), awe-inspiring jazz workouts, and alarming glimpses of life in the studio (like the "fast and bulbous" routine that introduces Pena).

A high point of creative insanity is reached during the musically sophisticated The Blimp, which opens with a complex high-speed drum and bass riff. Once established, it serves as backing to Beefheart's most deranged vocal tour de force, apparently phoned into the studio from some other location, in which he rants to Frank Zappa about the arrival of the mother ship that's going to make them all rich and famous. Disturbingly reminiscent of the radio commentary to the Hindenburg disaster, it's a draining and totally *un*easy-listening experience that epitomizes the whole magnificent album.

➲ We almost chose **Doc At The Radar Station**, Virgin, 1980

# Chemical Brothers

## Exit Planet Dust

Jbo/Freestyle Dust, 1995

Tom Rowlands and Ed Simmons (everything).

One of the most influential releases of the Nineties, the first Chemical Brothers album introduced electronica to a generation of guitar-fixated indie kids in the UK, and "broke" dance music in the US. The resulting cross-pollination has led to an exciting and reinvigorated rock scene on both sides of the Atlantic, while at the same time re-introducing a sense of the pace and the crowd-pleasing tricks of old-school rock to the dance scene.

Tom Rowlands and Ed Simmons met at Manchester University in 1989. Sharing an interest in hip-hop and DJ-ing, they set themselves up as the Dust Brothers in tribute to the US production team of the same name, a tag reflected in both the title **Exit Planet Dust** and the track In Dust We Trust. After six years building a reputation on the UK DJ and production scenes, however, the threat of legal action from their American heroes forced them to become the Chemical Brothers.

The Brothers' eclectic approach to choosing material when working as DJs saw them successfully blending the latest cutting-edge beats with cheesy Sixties instrumentals and forgotten pop hits. This mix-and-match approach was initially anathema at many purist club nights, but in time it grew popular enough to spawn the whole "Big Beat" scene. It also spilled over into Song To The Siren, the first ever Chemical Brothers track, which they recorded as a signature tune to play before DJ-ing other people's records. Such was the response that the pair moved towards exclusively playing their own music. Their exposure to mainstream rock audiences began as support act for Primal Scream on a 1994 tour, when they performed absolutely kicking – if not exactly visually exciting – gigs, lurking behind banks of rack-mounted technology, and brewing up a storm of hip-hop-influenced dance beats in sets that were every bit as tight as those of any conventional live band.

The Chemical Brothers formula consists of adding hip-hop beats and the dance sensibilities of classic house music to relatively conventional "rock" structures. Leave Home, previously released as a single, sets out the stall for the whole album with its "Brothers gonna work it out" sample (from Blake Baxter's original), clashing keyboard riffs, turntable trickery, and rumbling electronic percussion. It leads straight into "In Dust We Trust", followed by a live version of "Song To The Siren". That in turn kicks off a four-part sequence – continued through Three Little Birdies Down Beats, Fuck Up Beats and Chemical Beats – which closely mimics their pounding, ever-mounting live shows. The latin-tinged Chico's Groove, with its beautiful "gee, I don't know what's going on" sample, slows the pace right down, while One Too Many Mornings (not the Bob Dylan tune) is even more stately and dignified, with its cinematic sweep and gentle melancholy.

The Chemical Brothers' role as a bridge between dance and rock is exemplified by the appearance of indie-hero Tim Burgess of the Charlatans as guest vocalist on the standout Life Is Sweet. Swept along on a driving wave of keyboard noises, he somehow manages to cling on to a traditional verse/chorus song format. Playground For A Wedgeless Firm, a slow and menacing melding of synths, movie music and hip-hop, lumbers on like some enormous robot gone mad, paving the way for the intriguing climax of Alive Alone, in which Beth Orton's vocals are draped elegantly across a landscape of synthetic keyboards.

⊃ We almost chose **Dig Your Own Hole . . .**, Jbo/Freestyle Dust, 1997

# 22

# The Clash

## London Calling

Columbia, 1979

Joe Strummer (gtr, vocals), Mick Jones (gtr, pno, vocals), Paul Simonon (bass, vocals), Topper Headon (pcn, drums), Mick Gallagher (organ).

**London Calling** was effectively the last great punk album. Pointing out the many directions that alternative rock was free to take from then on, it confirmed the Clash as punk's most coherent and persuasive voice. It is nonetheless, a slice of pure combat rock, on which even the cover – a magnificent shot of Paul Simonon wielding his bass over his head like a sledgehammer – sets out to make a statement.

A double album, sold for the price of a low-budget single album, it was never going to earn huge money, but to regain the momentum generated by their epoch-defining first album, *The Clash* (and brush over the critical disaster of their second, *Give 'Em Enough Rope*), something exceptional was required. Pulling together as never before or since, the Clash delivered. London Calling itself, the album opener, is pure, uncluttered, urban paranoia, its woebegone vocals laid over swooping basslines and angry guitars. London's drowning and Joe lives by the river – so far, so angst-ridden, no surprises. But Brand New Cadillac – an old rock'n'roll number, respectfully treated by a punk band at a time when Teddy Boys (the UK's diehard defenders of old-school rock'n'roll) were still knocking lumps off punks just for daring to be on the street – was seen as saying something new. Jimmy Jazz – an unhurried r'n'b tale of cheeking the police and a snapshot view of big-city British life – boasts a catchy guitar riff and blossoms in the confident, brass-drenched production. It marks the first appearance on the album of the Clash's archetypal hero; the modern urban Robin Hood, on the run from the police and defending "the people" from "the man". He crops up again later in the London-reggae of Rudie Can't Fail and the braggadocio of Guns Of Brixton.

The Clash's earlier work had reflected their familiarity with the London punks' poisons of choice. Two albums and a few tours down the line, they were writing more thoughtful reflections of life in the fast lane, like Hateful, a well-drawn sketch of the love/hate relationship between client and supplier, and Koka Kola, a sly dig at cocaine use in musical, advertising and government circles. These days, even if they were so pilled up that they rattled (as claimed in Revolution Rock), they were dwelling less on the traditional working-class concern with the personal, and were readier to look at the big picture. In Spanish Bombs, clever imagery and a sad yet defiant melody combine to draw a parallel between the tragedy of the Spanish Civil War and the separatist struggles of the band's own era. Lost In The Supermarket uses stills from a suburban childhood and images of nervous collapse in a touchingly naive story of individual failure in the face of capital. Both are bold stabs at dealing with complex subjects and both, to a large extent, succeed.

Lovers Rock advocated safety and planning when it came to sweet loving, I'm Not Down was another battered, split-lip gesture of defiance, Four Horsemen was the male-bonding, self-mythologizing rock'n'roll epic of the Clash themselves, but the biggest treat was saved till last. Train In Vain, a last-minute throwaway story of love gone bad, didn't even make it onto the track listing on the original cover, yet it was the song that finally broke the band in the USA and made them a worldwide success.

Subsequent recordings never recaptured the magic of cheeky new ideas combined with rock'n'roll's gut feeling for a riff. International acclaim and hit singles notwithstanding, it was on *London Calling* that the Clash reached their peak.

➲ We almost chose **The Clash**, CBS, 1977

# 23

# Elvis Costello

## My Aim Is True

Stiff, 1977; reissued with bonus tracks Demon, 1993

Elvis Costello (gtr, pno, stick, vocals), John McFee (gtr), Sean Hopper (kbds), John Ciambotti (bass), Micky Shine (drums), Alex Call (gtr), Steve Nieve (kbds), Bruce Thomas (bass), Pete Thomas (drums), Andrew Bodnar (bass), Steve Goulding (drums), Nick Lowe (bass, piano, stick), Stan Shaw (organ).

Elvis Costello, who gave an eloquent voice to the tongue-tied UK punk movement, is one of the few veterans of the 1977 rush to stay on his feet, producing quality work into the Nineties. **My Aim Is True**, his first album, sparkled onto an already lively scene, raising the stakes through lyrics of unprecedented beauty and venom. Though the (for the times, dubious) distinction of comparison with Bob Dylan was there from the very beginning, Costello always veered more towards new-wave realism than to visions of dystopia.

Young Declan MacManus came from a musical family, and had previous experience through the band Flip City. Signed to the Stiff label on the strength of a couple of demos played on the radio show *Honky Tonk* (hosted by music guru Charlie Gillett), and hand-delivered to the record company offices, he cultivated a deranged geeky image that was half Buddy Holly, half Joe Strummer. Elvis Costello took London's punk scene apart, moving rapidly from music-press acclaim to mainstream recognition.

Recorded in 24 hours of snatched studio time for the even-then minuscule budget of £2000, and lightly produced by Nick Lowe, *My Aim Is True* is, for all the excellent, country-tinged efforts of McFee, Hopper, Ciambotti and Shine, recognizably the work of a single guy sitting alone with a guitar. Costello's uniquely vitriolic, albeit punk-influenced, songs dealt with emotional and personal themes, such as the bitter aftertaste left by the departure of a lover (covered in I'm Not Angry and Alison), as well as confidently treating bigger issues – resurgent street fascism in Less Than Zero, or the disguising of domestic violence in Watching The Detectives – with clever, punning lyrics and music that leaned at times more towards lightweight rock (as in Sneaky Feelings) than it did to conventional punk.

The sheer eclecticism of Costello's music won him a wide audience. While prepared to turn a basilisk new-wave stare on the ills of society, songs like (The Angels Wanna Wear My) Red Shoes and "Alison" draw more from the perfect pop of the Flamin' Groovies than they do from the urban squalor-rock of the Stooges. Similarly, Mystery Dance is little more than a speeded-up rock'n'roll riff, lifted straight from the late Fifties. Blame It On Cain bounces along chirpily enough, but elsewhere, when the subject matter suggests it, he experiments with ominous reggae rhythms and heartbroken, weedy, country'n'western twang. This technique of wrapping the unpleasantness in irresistibly catchy and intriguing tunes lifts the album's threatening gloom, although Costello's intense personal involvement with the more serious themes is beyond doubt.

Waiting For The End Of The World and "Watching The Detectives" have been bolted onto the CD reissue of the album, together with nine "pre-professional" demos that provide a glimpse of Costello's voice, and his earliest songs, still under development. While these latter undoubtedly offer a fuller picture of the artist, their main interest comes from their naivety.

My Aim Is True diverted the new wave from a blind alley of yobbish yells of defiance towards a more persuasive, discursive role. Costello himself went on to achieve international respect as a musician and commentator. Several of his later albums are more subtle and even better-crafted, but none approached the mould-breaking impact of his very first.

➲ We almost chose **Armed Forces**, Demon, 1979

# 24

# The Cure

## Mixed Up

Fiction, Elektra, 1990

Robert Smith (vocals, gtr, kbds), Simon Gallup (bass, kbds), Porl Thompson (gtr, kbds, sax), Laurence Tolhurst (kbds), Roger O'Donnell (kbds), Matthieu Hartley (kbds), Boris Williams (drums), Andy Anderson (drums), Phil Thornalley (bass), William Orbit (remixing), Paul Oakenfold (remixing).

From their 1978 debut single, "Killing An Arab" – introspective existentialism you could dance to – through to their sporadic broadsides of the Nineties, the Cure have produced some of the most impressive and enduring recordings in rock. During the early Eighties they were responsible for what, without doubt, rank among the bleakest and most negative outpourings of a decade that was characterized by the depression of its "serious" rock musicians. Then they blossomed, breaking the US market with the occasionally more whimsical *Kiss Me, Kiss Me, Kiss Me*. In the process, they moved away from their early, underground, "Gatwick sound", to evolve into the biggest festival and stadium attraction in the UK.

The Cure kicked off the Nineties with **Mixed Up**, a re-jigged-for-the-dancefloor collection of beats-plus-melancholia remixes that won back the waverers in their indie-kid audience, and also brought them to the attention of the dance crowd. This radical reassessment of their gloomy back catalogue – compiled from tracks originally heard on *Seventeen Seconds* (1980), *The Top* (1984), *Head On The Door* (1985), *Kiss Me . . .* (1987), and *Disintegration* (1989) – stunned and alienated their more conservative Goth supporters, but won them widespread respect for their bravery. *Mixed Up* arrived in the middle of that brief moment when rock and beats combined to produce genuinely exciting and inventive hybrids, before the dance world fell prey to its own set of conformities and prejudice.

The Cure had never been short of ideas, and the album drew on their entire staggering range. Most of the tracks were worked on by Robert Smith and Mark Saunders, who used a rock vocabulary to bridge the gap between the plodding "disco remixes" of the Eighties and the masterpiece re-interpretations of today. These reworkings tend to be comparatively non-interventionist – an extra emphasis to the drum beat, the judicious addition of reverb to the vocals, some looping keyboard flourishes – but they have remarkable results. Lullaby, for example, a song of nightmare in its original version, gains in eeriness through a three-minute instrumental introduction. The cold landscape of Fascination Street is chillier in the remix, while the bleak despair of Pictures Of You turns to a contemplative and more bearable feeling of regret, thanks to a new shuffling beat.

The standout tracks, however, are the ones that received the professional touch. In the album's boldest revamp, William Orbit takes Inbetween Days into uncharted territory, adding laid-back drums, keyboard samples that stutter and fade, and snatches of percussive vocals, while Paul Oakenfold put together the mix of Close To Me that carried the Cure to the clubs. Building on outrageously fat beats, he boosted the brass and recycled Smith's breathless vocals to make a sunny Sunday-cruising theme which, like much here, has aged far better than the original.

Ironically, while the Cure's conventional albums are themselves self-contained, with their own doom-laden sincerity and cohesion, Robert Smith and the band are best at compressing ideas into the confined space of a single track; call it musical agoraphobia, whatever, it seems to work. The individual cuts of *Mixed Up*, taken out of context, re-faceted and re-interpreted through dub techniques that focus attention on previously insignificant phrases, stand as their most powerful anthology.

➲ We almost chose **Kiss Me, Kiss Me, Kiss Me**, Fiction, 1987

# 25

# Dead Kennedys

## Fresh Fruit for Rotting Vegetables

Alternative Tentacles, 1980

Jello Biafra (vocals), Klaus Flouride (bass, vocals), Paul Roessler (kbds), East Bay Ray (gtr), Ninotchka (kbds), Ray Papperell (gtr), D H Phillegro (drums).

American punk rock was largely the sound of spoiled brats (or at least kids who wanted to be spoiled) having temper tantrums because the consumer paradise wasn't all it was cracked up to be. While their fellow snot-noses in Southern California were complaining that they couldn't get laid, that fast food sucked, that there was nothing on TV, and that the in-crowd jocks kept beating them up, San Francisco's Dead Kennedys pictured themselves as the world's most committed anti-fascists, and became left-wing superheroes.

In their crusade against the bourgeoisie, the Dead Kennedys' main weapon was sarcasm. Unfortunately, sarcasm was also their kryptonite. They seemed unable to do anything but make snide remarks at all-too-obvious targets, and their caustic side tended to creep into their music with grating, nyah-nyah-nyah guitar lines. But punk's main pleasure was its cathartic blast of self-righteousness, and few bands pushed those buttons so well.

Their 1979 vinyl debut, the single California über Alles, was a near-perfect skewering of California's hippy blight and its collapse into new-age cultishness. Lines like "You will jog for the master race / And always wear the happy face", "Mellow out or you will pay" and "It's the suede-denim secret police / They have come for your uncool niece" savaged pop's image of the Golden State as a heaven on earth, and pointed out that hippy culture was really conservatism dressed in Guatemalan sweaters, Birkenstocks and beards.

The next single, Holiday in Cambodia, was even better. A brutal parody of the condescension and contradictions of white liberalism, "Holiday in Cambodia" was the retort that Norman Mailer's "The White Negro" and Jane Fonda deserved. Crucially, with its ominous bass roil and tense guitar figures, it was also one of the few times that the DKs' music matched Biafra's wit. Both of these singles (albeit in slightly different versions) appear on the first of their six albums, **Fresh Fruit For Rotting Vegetables**. While they're clearly its best moments, several other songs on the album are worth waiting around for, and overall it's their funniest and least puerile effort.

Kicking off with Kill the Poor's sterling couplet, "Efficiency and progress is ours once more now that we have the neutron bomb / It's quick and clean and gets things done", *Fresh Fruit* proceeds to depict a post-nuclear utopia of ever-escalating property values and slum-free living. Other gloriously idiotic gems include the infanticidal anthems, I Kill Children and Funland at the Beach – which has the priceless line, "See the crushed little kids adorn the boardwalk"– and their piss-take of Viva Las Vegas which cries out for a computer-enhanced video of Biafra shimmying with Ann-Margret. Their strange relationship with old-fashioned rock'n'roll continues on Stealing People's Mail, a punked-up version of Chuck Berry's "Round and Round". Let's Lynch the Landlord, meanwhile, stole its bassline from the Blues Magoos' garage classic, "We Ain't Got Nothin' Yet".

Despite highlights like *Nazi Punks Fuck Off* and *Too Drunk to Fuck*, the later DK albums were a series of diminishing returns in parallel with the general demise of the punk movement. Though the band broke up in 1986 after accumulating huge legal bills trying to fight a lawsuit that contended the insert of H. R. Giger's "Penis Landscape" in their *Frankenchrist* album violated community standards of decency, Jello Biafra crusades on as a First Amendment warrior and spoken-word artist.

➲ We almost chose **Give Me Convenience . . .**, Alternative Tentacles, 1987

# 26

# Dexys Midnight Runners

## Searching For The Young Soul Rebels

EMI, 1980

Kevin Rowland (vocals, gtr), Al Archer (gtr), Andy Growcott (organ), Pete Saunders (organ), Mick Talbot (organ), Jeff Blythe (tenor sax), Pete Williams (bass), Steve "Babyface" Spooner (alto sax), Big Jimmy Paterson (trombone), Bobby Junior (drums).

Risen from the ashes of Birmingham punks the Killjoys, Dexys Midnight Runners turned towards the Stax soul scene of Memphis. In this, their first incarnation, they sought a more positive direction that would incorporate the sheer intensity of soul music into the frenetic emotional rush and anger of punk. Their first single, "Dance Stance", showcased this "pure passion" approach, systematically challenging and pulling down blocks of anti-Irish prejudice with a marvellous chanted backing vocal during the chorus that comprised a list of Irish writers from Oscar Wilde to Edna O'Brien.

"Dance Stance" served as a taster for Dexys' much-anticipated first album, **Searching For The Young Soul Rebels**, for which it was re-recorded as Burn It Down. Here it bursts open – after a naive but effective introduction in which a radio skims between stations, catching snippets of "Smoke On The Water", "Holidays In The Sun", and "Working For The Rat Race" – with a brief call-and-response team-building yell and a blast of brass that echoes the finest and tightest of the US soul bands. Kevin Rowland's instantly recognizable (and much mimicked) voice yodels and wails in a pre-Commitments appropriation of soul as the voice of the oppressed, no matter what colour they may be.

Following Rowland's initial conception, Dexys attempted to meld rebellion, socialism and bad behaviour, with sleevenotes presenting the band as a criminal gang who are planning a "caper". Quoting from Brendan Behan's *Borstal Boy*, and drawing also on Scorsese's *Mean Streets*, they gave bad-boy track titles even to gorgeous instrumentals such as The Teams That Meet In Caffs, on which they sound like a sadder, wiser Booker T and the MGs. There's a touch of Jackie Wilson in the impressively titled Thankfully Not Living In Yorkshire It Doesn't Apply, but it's hidden behind Rowland's most exaggerated vocal pyrotechnics of the entire album – so wracked with soul, so drenched in feeling, that you can't make out a word of it.

The anger outweighs the soul in Tell Me When My Light Turns Green, though it's Rowland's too-much too-young lyrics ("seen quite a bit in my 23 years" and "spat on and shat on", for example) that stay in the mind. The venom spills out again in Keep It, a snipe at stay-at-home revolutionaries.

The first of the two real standout tracks, the instantly appealing Geno, finished side one back in the days of vinyl. Looking back to 1968, when Geno Washington was burning up the clubs of Britain with his storming soul revue, it went to number one in the charts. Another faux-Stax stomper, it's echoed in the climactic poison-pen soul of There, There, My Dear. Rushing centre-stage in a flurry of tight brass trills and pounding guitar-drum bravado, that final cut allows Rowland full rein to preen outrageously through lyrics of contempt such as "you're like some dumb, dumb patriot" and armchair anarchism like "the only way to change things is to shoot men who arrange things".

Despite a name that saluted Dexedrine – Smith, Klein & French's pep pill, the illicit drug of choice on the Sixties mod scene in Britain – Dexys maintained a strict anti-booze and drugs policy, in the hope of focusing energies that might otherwise have been dissipated. On *Young Soul Rebels*, it paid off; their taut, disciplined arrangements and heart-stirring soul produced some of the Eighties' most inventive and memorable music.

➲ We almost chose **Too-Rye-Ay**, Phonogram/Mercury, 1982

# 27

# The Doors

## The Doors

Elektra, 1967

Jim Morrison (vocals), Ray Manzarek (organ, pno, kbds), Robbie Krieger (gtr), John Densmore (drums).

With its sparse, uncomplicated arrangements and brooding atmosphere, the Doors' first album might have been recorded yesterday. It's a timeless album on which the very un-churchlike organ, precise guitar work, and restrained, jazz-tinged drumming provide a menacing backup to the throaty, randy vocals. Add in Jim Morrison's onstage shaman antics, his bad-boy good looks, and a wholesale embracing of the psychedelic lifestyle, and you have the first hippy Elvis, full of pheromones and hallucinogens, and come for your children and all you hold dear.

By the time **The Doors** came out, the band themselves were already "stoned, immaculate" veterans and heroes of the clubs on Sunset Strip. Helped in part, no doubt, by the West Coast stoner lifestyle, they managed to devote a year to getting the set together before they entered the studios. They could draw on a wider and, frankly, classier range of influences than most of their peers; both Morrison and Ray Manzarek had attended UCLA film school, while Manzarek was also a classically trained pianist with a passion for rhythm'n'blues; Robby Krieger's playing and writing were informed by a deep love of Chicago blues, classical and flamenco guitar; and John Densmore brought the best elements of freestyle jazz to his drumming. Morrison had a flair for writing gloomy, lovesick poetry that, laid over Krieger's well-crafted music, became transformed into great lyrics, and created a new, interesting, challenging rock'n'roll. It was sexy, you could dance to it, the singer wore very tight pants, your parents hated it, and you could argue all night long about the words. It was a hit with the hipsters and cool with the kids.

Break On Through, the first track, reveals a set of brainy dopers who have delved into the occult and returned with eye-popping accounts of what lies on "the other side", depicting a world of lost children talking through the night as they "learn to forget". Twentieth Century Fox, a more conventional portrait of a dream girl, lightens the mood, and serves to cleanse the palate before the Brecht/Weill composition Alabama Song, a chilling cry of hedonism and amorality that reads as a tribute from the doom-sayers of the love generation to their elders.

Light My Fire, the grandstand number that closes the first side of the original album, opens with the most famous keyboard line since "Green Onions", and grows into the Sixties' greatest celebration of stoned love. A lustier, in-your-face variant of the "song plus meandering solo" acid-rock formula then blossoming at Pink Floyd gigs in London, it was finally released as a single – cut down to a manageable length – and took the Doors world-wide.

Apart from the macho bravado of Back Door Man, there's little to lighten the second half of the album. The regret at lost opportunity of I Looked at You, the black-leather Blake of End Of The Night and the veiled warnings of Take It As It Comes stretch like a dark corridor towards the massive, atmospheric, motherfucking epic: The End.

Thirty years down the line, "The End" remains a richly structured, brave attempt to deal with the complex Oedipus myth. Gently exploding swells of keyboards support lyrics of scattered, fragmented imagery that, whether acid-induced or culled from high culture, still generate thrills. Although the "weird scenes" were to continue for the Doors for another three years, nothing until Jim's death had the power of this first statement.

➲ We almost chose **Morrison Hotel**, Elektra, 1970

# 28

# Nick Drake

## Bryter Later

Island/Rykodisc/Hannibal, 1970

Nick Drake (gtr, pno, vocals), John Cale (kbds, cello, viola), Richard Thompson (gtr),
Chris McGregor (pno, vocals), Lyn Dobson (flute), Ray Warleigh (flute), Dave Pegg
(bass), Ed Carter (bass), Paul Harris (pno), Robert Kirby (strings), Mike Kowalski
(drums), Dave Mattacks (drums).

Perhaps the most famous "unknown" artist in popular music, Nick Drake was the greatest British singer-songwriter. A darker, more mature Donovan, he delivered his chilling, melancholy songs in a captivating, husky voice, the lyrics densely packed with scurrying ideas. His elegant tunes were adorned with novel chord changes, classy hooks, and changes of pace that won him the respect and collaboration of his fellow musicians, while his unique blend of psychedelic imagery and tranquillizing vocals have endeared him to a devoted cult audience ever since his tragic death in 1974, aged only 26.

In **Bryter Later**, his second album, Nick Drake created a heartfelt set of songs, trimmed of all frills and self-indulgence. Contrasting with the slightly overdone lushness of his debut, *Five Leaves Left*, and the unremitting bleakness of his third and final full-length recording, *Pink Moon*, *Bryter Later* achieved a perfect balance between Drake's understated lyrical style and the sumptuous string arrangements of his college friend Rob Kirby.

Drake started writing songs at school, but it was at Cambridge University that he picked up his trademark all-in-black look and taste for smoking dope. Signing up with Fairport Convention producer Joe Boyd, he dropped out and recorded *Five Leaves Left* in 1968. It received excellent reviews, but he found performing live almost unbearable, and the tour that followed was a disaster.

*Bryter Later*, cut after he'd moved to London, was Drake's most upbeat recording. In particular, it boasts a trio of skilful, almost cheery, instrumentals: Introduction, all nifty fingerpicking and swooning strings; Bryter Later itself, a weather forecast for the psyche, with its pastoral flute melodies and masterful chord progression; and the closer Sunday, which reprises the flute theme, laid over a delicate guitar and string arrangement. The tongue-in-cheek Poor Boy, too, despite its repeated lyrical theme that "nobody sees . . . cares . . . smiles", is lifted by the incongruous female backing vocals ("Oh poor boy, so sorry for himself / Oh poor boy, so worried for his health"), the marvellous saxophone lines, and the complex Latin rhythm.

Both Hazey Jane II and Hazey Jane I (which appear in that order) are wistful songs of love, on which Drake's voice grows more husky, the brass instruments quietly sob, and the percussion rises and falls like the wings of a seabird in slow motion. By contrast, the city – seen as menacing, dark and impersonal – is the villain in At The Chime Of The City Clock, with its ominous descending chords and sax trills. While all these songs lift into refrains of breathtaking beauty, it's on Northern Sky that everything comes totally together. As Drake becomes increasingly involved in the lyric, this magnificent piece builds from a restrained, slow-burning background, to a climactic swell of almost-sanctified organ and a vocal line of aching commitment.

Nick Drake was the archetypal hippy singer-songwriter, and was thrown into despair that despite his soul-baring sincerity, utterly unblemished by cynicism, his music failed to sell. His reluctance to tour did little to help, and he swiftly passed through breakdown to the virtual incoherence of *Pink Moon* and, beyond that, to his death, following an overdose. His albums, however, have never been out of print, and they've continued to influence succeeding generations of songwriters, from Elvis Costello to the thoughtful alternative rockers of the Nineties.

➲ We almost chose **Pink Moon**, Island, 1972

# Bob Dylan

## Bringing It All Back Home

CBS, 1965

Bob Dylan (gtr, harmonica, kbds, vocals), John Hammond, Jr. (gtr), John Sebastian (bass), Kenny Rankin (gtr), John Boone (bass), Bobby Gregg (drums).

Forget the rest, this is the one. The album that re-defined rock-'n'roll, that infused it with poetry, that made it intelligent. And all shot through with a sparkling sense of humour that left no doubt that Dylan was having the last laugh. **Bringing It All Back Home** confronted the shallowness of pop and the complacency of society, all the while holding up a surrealist distorting mirror to modern life.

Dylan's first electric album – although he had experimented with an electric sound as early as 1962 with his first single, "Mixed-Up Confusion" – horrified his more traditional folk followers. Inspired by the Beatles, whom he met (and turned on to dope) in the summer of 1964 – "I knew they were pointing the direction of where music had to go" – Dylan set about harnessing his various influences – Woody Guthrie, William Blake, Rimbaud, Ginsberg and Kerouac – to a driving rock beat.

The results were astounding. In the intensely creative burst that started with *Bringing It All Back Home* in 1965, Dylan swiftly followed up with two further LPs of stunning ambition and substance, *Highway 61 Revisited* and *Blonde on Blonde*. Blurring the distinctions between rock'n'roll and poetry, pop and protest, this trilogy placed the lone singer-songwriter centre-stage, as a prime mover in the seismic changes being experienced by western society. Sure, there are the usual things to annoy the casual Dylan listener – the nasal whine, the ropey harmonica, the tinny organ – but the flood of ideas in these three albums elevates them to a seminal position in postwar culture.

If *Bringing It All Back Home* had contained no more than Subterranean Homesick Blues, its place in modem history would still be assured. In just over two minutes of dazzling lyrical pyrotechnics, the song overwhelms the listener with its quick-fire imagery and relentless sloganeering. Aphorisms like "You don't need to be a weatherman to know which way the wind blows" have entered mainstream consciousness, even as they declaim the absurdity of mainstream life where after "twenty years of schooling . . . they put you on the day shift".

It's Alright, Ma (I'm Only Bleeding), a caustic, stream-of-consciousness attack on consumerism, packs a similarly powerful punch. "Money doesn't talk, it swears", and while advertising cons you into buying "everything from toy guns that spark / to flesh-coloured Christs that glow in the dark / it's easy to see without looking too far that nothing's really sacred". Maggie's Farm takes things a stage further, brutally ridiculing mass production and the whole capitalist structure of labour relations.

The album's two devotional love songs, She Belongs To Me and Love Minus Zero/No Limit, were probably inspired respectively by Dylan's ex-lover, Joan Baez, and by Sara Lowndes, whom he was secretly to marry in November 1965. It was Sara who introduced him to film-maker Donn Pennebaker, who captured his 1965 UK tour in "Don't Look Back", a documentary that unforgettably opens with Dylan frantically holding up placards of key phrases from "Subterranean Homesick Blues" in time with the music.

The break-up of his relationship with Baez was also the inspiration for It's All Over Now, Baby Blue, the album's final track, and, despite its air of sadness and resignation, one of Dylan's most accessible tunes. *Bringing It All Back Home* was Dylan's first million-seller. At the time he was 24. Look on his works, ye mighty, and despair.

➲ We almost chose **Blonde on Blonde**, CBS, 1966

# 30

# Echo and the Bunnymen

## Crocodiles

Korova/Warner, 1980

Ian McCulloch (vocals, gtr), Will Sergeant (gtr), Les Pattinson (bass), Pete De Freitas (drums), David Balfe (kbds).

Formed from a distillation of Liverpool's bitchy, incestuous art-school and punk-rock scenes, Echo And The Bunnymen first came together to play as support to The Teardrop Explodes at Eric's, the city's famed nightclub – possibly the most extreme combination of ridiculous band names ever seen. By the time they'd put together enough of a set for **Crocodiles**, their debut album, founder member Echo – the drum machine – had left the band, to be replaced by the more amenable De Freitas. Thanks to Mac and Sergeant, Echo And The Bunnymen strode boldly away from the stagnant pool of punk, in the darkly psychedelic direction that had first been indicated by the Thirteenth Floor Elevators, the Electric Prunes, and their US garage-band peers back in the Sixties.

At the time the Bunnymen were playing their first gigs, some extraordinarily powerful LSD was circulating throughout the UK. Liverpool was no exception, and while the band members themselves weren't known for dabbling beyond the doors of perception, many in their circle of friends undoubtedly did. This had a profound effect upon their songs. From their first singles onwards – the fragile, accusatory Pictures On My Wall and the more robust Rescue (both included on *Crocodiles*) – the band helped to create a new British psychedelia, far bleaker than that of the more optimistic Sixties. Characterized by chiming melodic guitars, solemn basslines and arty lyrics, their music drips with a damp, cold misery suited to the dank British climate, as well as the overwhelming gloom that pervaded "serious" rock music in the early Eighties.

Moving straight from punk to psychedelic rock led to some interesting mixtures of musical influences. *Crocodiles* opens, for example, with an intro borrowed from the Hawkwind songbook and a Roky Erikson-inspired "Up, up, up" lyric, the whole thing stirred up with lashings of reverb and an echoing, roomy mix. Monkeys too blends a twinkling, distant, space-guitar sound, remembered from San Francisco's acid-rock explosion, with sneery, late-punk lyrics, while Villiers Terrace combines the doomy intoned vocals of Joy Division and the dispassionate cinema-verité recording of drugs and degradation of the Velvet Underground atop a glam-rock chord progression.

The Bunnymen excelled at fast, paranoid rockers with wilfully obscure lyrics such as Crocodiles, Rescue – with its nervous, disjointed, double-tracked vocals, and sense of self-doubt and fear – and the overtly "trippy" Pictures On My Wall, starring Mac's dark-eyed lost boy who's "loving it all" as it matches Siouxsie and the Banshees for sheer horror-movie atmospherics.

*Crocodiles* created an enormous stir in the UK. While Mac's "pouting superstar" good looks won them poster space in teenagers' bedrooms, the band's unsmiling delivery and angst-ridden lyrics scored with tortured adolescents and tormented students everywhere. Picking up massive press coverage, in part through McCulloch's naive remarks on rock music and life in general, they swiftly became the country's premier live band. A generation of art students grew their hair shaggy, developed fetching pouts, and loomed around in shin-length overcoats.

One of the first albums to draw attention to the early-Eighties scene in northern England, *Crocodiles* made the Bunnymen such stars that they dominated the British music scene for most of the decade, inspiring acts as diverse as stadium-fillers U2 or Simple Minds, to five-minute-pop-wonders like Big Country.

➲ We almost chose **Songs To Learn And Sing**, Sire, 1985

# 31

# Brian Eno

## Here Come The Warm Jets

EG, 1973

Brian Eno (synth,gtr, kbds, vocals), Robert Fripp (gtr), Phil Manzanera (gtr), John Wetton (bass, gtr), Chris Spedding (gtr), Busta Cherry Jones (bass), Simon King (pcn), Bill MacCormick (bass), Andy MacKay (kbds, sax).

More than just one of rock music's strangest titles – it's said to be a reference to urination – **Here Come The Warm Jets** is one of its most influential albums. It established Brian Eno as an artist in his own right after two years' hard labour in Roxy Music, manipulating noise-generating gadgetry, festooned in glam-rock glad-rags like some crazed "drag telephonist". The important element of insanity had gone, there had been a falling out with the band's other eye-catching attraction, Brian Ferry, and frankly, Eno was ready for a little fun.

Eno had been working with tape recorders since his Sixties' stint at art school, where he'd formed an avant-garde performance group, and had a profound interest in experimental composers like La Monte Young and John Cage. That made an ideal background for his first post-Roxy outing, *No Pussyfooting*, on which he shared the credits with guitar-revolutionary Robert Fripp, then working with King Crimson. For his solo project, however, Eno harked back to the best parts of his glam-rock superstar past, creating a lighter, art-pop sound and seeking more to entertain than to astound. A smash-and-grab raid that rescued the synthesizer from the cerebral, progressive rock camp, it opened the way for the vibrant electro-pop of the latter half of the Seventies.

Several tracks hint at Eno's subsequent move towards longer, ambient pieces. Thus Cindy Tells Me is a spacey pop cruise with a gorgeous backing chorus, On Some Faraway Beach has a three-minute instrumental wall-of-sound introduction, and Remember Me brings in long drawn-out, droning backing vocals and an extended slide guitar theme. The final track, Here Come The Warm Jets itself, offers an even clearer glimpse of his future, with its repeated, driving fuzzed-up guitar riff, occasionally coloured with hints of tubular bells deep in the mix; the introduction of percussion, almost as an afterthought, midway through the track; and the way the vocals are used as simply one more instrument.

Elsewhere, Eno creates stomping pop music; opening track Needle In The Camel's Eye starts like a glam remake of the Velvet Underground's "Waiting For The Man" (Eno was a fan), complete with mischievous Duane Eddy-style guitar break, while for Paw Paw Negro Blowtorch he opts for camp vocal delivery and a funny "squelchy" synth break that would have been at home on an animated kids' TV show. The quirkiest and most amusing cut of all is Dead Finks Don't Talk, a gently paced, superficially straightforward pop song on which nonsense like "Oh cheeky, cheeky, Oh naughty, sneaky" is chanted in tongue-in-cheek, high-camp tones, while crazed backing vocalists shriek "Oh no!" over and over again.

Not everything is sweetness and light, however. The sinister lyrics of Baby's On Fire are sung with crystal clarity, while extra menace comes from the ritualistic drumming and the slashing guitar work that takes up most of its five minutes. The upsetting Driving Me Backwards is essentially a slow, neurotic, insistent piano riff, festooned with distorted guitar, over which a clearly disturbed Eno wails of doom and portent. Blank Frank, variously agreed to be a poison-pen portrait of either a gangster or a well-known glam-pop band's lead vocalist who shared the same initials, uses a muddy, Bo Diddley-esque riff to impart verses that drip with venom and spite.

➲ We almost chose **My Life in the Bush of Ghosts**, Virgin/Sire, 1981

# 32

# Marianne Faithfull

## Broken English

Island, 1979

Marianne Faithfull (vocals), Steve Winwood (gtr), Steve York (bass), Darryl Way (violin), Terry Stannard (drums).

Like some post-punk fairy godmother, Marianne Faithfull suffered for her sins and came back, grizzled and bloodied, to tell the tale. By the late Seventies, she had been rehabilitated, thanks to harrowing confessions of debauchery, from her pre-punk image as spoiled rock-star's girlfriend to be hailed as a cool veteran of the drug wars. A female equivalent of Keith Richards, still happily puffing on a cigarette and swigging vodka, Faithfull had in the process developed one of the great white-soul voices, toughened by experience and hard knocks, and perfectly tuned for the spectrum of emotions that stretch between lust and anger.

For the best part of a decade, since the prophetic "Sister Morphine" single of 1969, Marianne been all but lost in a narcotic haze. She seemed finally to have been dragged down by the tensions of being forever dismissed as simply Mick Jagger's partner, despite the hints of hidden depths evident even in early singles such as her breathy, existential version of the Stones' "As Tears Go By". In the twelve months following its release, she went through a series of personal catastrophes, ending up as a recluse and a junkie. There was a comeback album in 1977, *Faithless*, but that proved to be a false start, vanishing without trace and offering little indication of the sheer power and conviction of what was to follow.

By the time she recorded *Broken English*, Faithfull had embraced the hard-edged attitudes of punk, and seized upon the new directions that were now opening up for female vocalists. Pulling a band together that included Sixties legend Steve Winwood on guitar, she assembled a set of haunting originals and intriguing cover versions that would draw praise from the critics, achieve high sales, and even earn a compliment from Bob Dylan.

With its up-to-the-minute production values and sharp, night-club rhythms, the album sounded as cool as it looked, in a blue-on-blue sleeve lit only by the cigarette in Faithfull's hand. From the title track Broken English onwards, which showcased her scarred and splintered, drained-of-emotion voice over a prowling electronic beat, it was clear that we were in the presence of Grace Jones' seriously pissed-off big sister.

The pagan-inspired rites of Witches Song placed ancient ritual next to modern notions of sisterhood in a sublime, cruising guitar rocker that drew parallels between the wise women of the past and the informed and aware women of today. Brain Drain, on the other hand, is a far darker urban funk number, with a night-time riff and a nightmare subject: how to deal with a partner who is just as much of a lying, thieving junkie as yourself. Elsewhere, though Faithfull and the band explore reggae rhythms and bouncy funk-rock as means of delivery, the message itself remains unremittingly bleak.

Covers like the bitter Ballad Of Lucy Jordan – the Dr Hook song – and a faster, march-paced version of John Lennon's Working Class Hero are radical reinterpretations of the originals, poignant and heartfelt. The real standout, however, is the final cut, Why D'Ya Do It, which uses an angry reggae beat to support vulgar lyrics of degradation and vitriol. A six-and-a-half-minute, coarse-mouthed epic diatribe ("Why d'ya spit on my snatch?" is one of its milder lines), sparked by betrayal, it showcases Faithfull in a spell-binding bravura performance, seething, snarling and dangerous.

➲ We almost chose **Strange Weather**, Island, 1987

# 33

# The Fall

## Grotesque (after the gramme)

Rough Trade, 1980

Mark E. Smith (vocals, vox organ), Marc Riley (bass, gtr, kbds), Steve Hanley (bass), Craig Scanlon (gtr), Karl Burns (drums), Paul Hanley (drums), Mike Leigh (drums).

The Fall have issued at least an album per year since 1978, and their indisputable influence on the punk and indie scenes on both sides of the Atlantic stems more from the accumulated impact of two decades in the avant-garde than from any specific release. **Grotesque** is however among the Fall's most powerful statements, and was recorded by the most inventive of the band's constantly evolving line-ups. Rapidly outgrowing the conventional definition of a punk combo, the Fall created a dark, disjointed, at times swaggering sound that looked for inspiration beyond plain vanilla rock'n'roll to the stranger flavours of Can and the Velvet Underground. The music has always been challenging, there are no lyric sheets to crib from, and Smith's delivery of them is characterized by a strong Manchester accent. You need to work at it.

1980 was the year when the Fall really got into their stride. The speed-driven paranoia of their first two albums had given way to an edgy, tense, yet self-confident music to support Smith's newly matured venom, and they kicked off the new decade with three challenging singles. The music veered from slow and ominous one- or two-chord riffs through to "Mancabilly", a diseased, rocking rhythm that Smith himself described as "Country'n'Northern". These new songs revealed him to be a bitter caricaturist who, like Hogarth, used his art to reveal the sleaze and brutishness of the British underclass. Thus Container Drivers shatters the stereotype of the noble trucker, depicting a world of loudmouthed ignorance and bowel-rotting gluttony; Pay Your Rates excoriates small-minded conformity; and In The Dark tells of sordid al fresco sex in the chilly twilight.

The Fall had moved away from the constrictions of the three-minute snapshot song format of standard punk. To build up a more complex emotional atmosphere takes time, and *Grotesque* features several longer pieces, like New Face In Hell and The NWRA (i.e. The North Will Rise Again), on which themes are explored in more detail. The first is a paranoid tale of sinister government agencies "disappearing" innocent amateur radio hams, the second an epic vision of rebellion doomed to failure.

Other songs are crammed with enormous detail and multi-layered stories. For example, C'n'C'-Smithering begins as a steadily paced, if oblique, history of the band, starting with a gig played at a cash'n'carry company's staff party, then moving on to tricks played on engineers at early recording sessions, and a meeting with "Big A&M Herb" Alpert. While Smith grows progressively more enraged, the song takes on and dismisses the group's musical contemporaries, sneers at their shameless pursuit of big-time success, and features a poisonous sketch of sexual violence on mainstream television. Impression of J. Temperance is a stark, mud-stained tale of cloning gone horribly wrong, while Gramme Friday is a Thursday-morning come-down hymn to amphetamines, that also draws in the willingness of Hitler's personal physician to prescribe the Führer something for the weekend. Elsewhere, as in W.M.C. Blob 59, fragments of taped rehearsals and conversation flutter in and out of the mix, adding to that sense of everything being on the brink of collapse into mayhem that had become the Fall's trademark.

Deep down, Mark E. Smith is a romantic who'd rather not articulate his vision of utopia, and prefers to illuminate the gloom and injustice of everyday life. *Grotesque* may be far from easy listening, but that's exactly what the band had in mind.

➲ We almost chose **Hex Enduction Hour**, Cog Sinister, 1982

# Gang Of Four

## Entertainment!

EMI, 1979

Dave Allen (bass), Hugo Burnham (drums), Andy Gill (gtr), Jon King (vocals).

A passionately angry, defiantly Marxist, intellectual post-punk rock band comprising three university students and a lorry driver was never going to deliver lightweight, good-time, party music. The Gang Of Four – who took their name from the ultra-leftist Chinese clique responsible for the Cultural Revolution – developed a powerful, rhythmic sound as a means to drive home their political messages without descending into bombast. While Gill was reviving the lost art of longdrawn-out feedback and sabre-like guitar angst, King declaimed sparse urgent lyrics over the verge-of-funk rhythms produced by Allen (whose bass effectively functioned as another lead guitar) and Burnham's Boys'-Brigade, paramilitary drumming.

Gill and King shared the limelight, combining outrageous feedback yowls and clashing, shimmering discords with lyrics that foretold doom for the complacent bourgeoisie. Disdaining conventional love songs, the Gang Of Four focused their attentions on repression, materialism, and the impossibility of true love in a world where the workers have yet to control the means of production. Reissued with three bonus tracks recorded after the completion of the original album, **Entertainment!** jumpstarted the British white-funk scene, and challenged the political apathy of punk.

On the strength of their debut EP, *Damaged Goods* – released on the fiercely independent Scottish label Fast Product, and later included, along with some fascinating early Human League tracks, on that label's full-length compilation – the Gang of Four were signed to EMI, prompting inevitable accusations that they were "selling out". Two of those early cuts were re-recorded for inclusion on this, their first album. The Situationist slogans and anti-capitalist motifs of the sleeve were impressive enough, but the subversive bluntness of the lyrics and the unrestrained rhythms made *Entertainment!* an instant hit with the radical dance-oriented sector.

Bursting with raw intensity from start to finish, the album opens with Ether, which tackles the extremely controversial topic (for an English band) of the British army's ill-treatment of detainees in the notorious H-Block prison camps of Northern Ireland. Natural's Not In It and Return The Gift give a funked-up once-over to materialism, the evils of direct marketing, and the "problem" of what to do with leisure time, while Not Great Men attempts to rewrite the history books, reappraising their fascination with ancient heroes by means of a great pop hook.

Anthrax stuns with its awesome, inspired feedback guitar intro and sharp, cold glare at love as product. With a tip of the hat to the Velvet Underground, the vocals on one channel chant a story of confusion and sickness, in which love is portrayed as a disease, while the other carries a diatribe against the very notion of love as a topic for pop songs. Damaged Goods is a powerful tale of dysfunctional, sweaty sex, with the feedback reprised on I Found That Essence Rare – an all-out rant against the propaganda role of the mainstream media – and At Home He's A Tourist, which is characterized by galloping drum and bass behind fiercely arrhythmic guitar chops.

The sharp, angular music and unrestrained politics of *Entertainment!* paved the way for revolutionary musicians like This Heat, the Pop Group, the Redskins, and the Jesus And Mary Chain, and went on to win praise from such luminaries as Michael Stipe and Kurt Cobain.

➲ We almost chose **A Brief History of the 20th Century**, EMI, 1990

# 35

# Happy Mondays

## Pills'n'Thrills and Bellyaches

Factory, 1990

Shaun Ryder (vocals), Paul Davis (kbds), Mark Berry (pcn), Guitar Day (gtr), Paul Ryder (bass), Gary Whelan (drums).

It gradually came to be accepted at the end of the Eighties that, given the right combination of music and drugs, white boys could indeed funk. That was the point when the Happy Mondays emerged as Manchester's prime groovers, speaking directly to Thatcher's children: the law-ignoring, chemical underground. For a few short months, ecstasy turned the beer-drenched macho world of indie music into a street party. All of a sudden, hitherto straightforward rock bands turned to Sly And The Family Stone for inspiration, and developed a new willingness to relax and let the music flow.

**Pills'n'Thrills and Bellyaches** was "Madchester" at its peak, but the Mondays had been there since the beginning. On their third and biggest-selling album, the drugs were still working, the band was a major success, and everything in the garden seemed totally chilled. There was more than just a groove going for the Mondays' music, however. Shaun Ryder's been-there-done-that vocals, forever suggesting that he was finding it just a bit too difficult to maintain concentration, welded an air of excess and sleaze onto the basic sound. Shaun always sounded like he'd taken more, stayed up for longer, and had seen more shocking sights than the rest; his postcards always came from the edge.

As Shaun and the boys – a bunch of genuine low-life street villains – celebrated good old-fashioned rock'n'roll hedonism, their music glowed with self-confidence. It would all turn most sour very shortly, but for one brief moment, apart from a noticeable wheeze in Shaun's vocals and blanker than usual expressions from the rest of the band, the Mondays were on top of the world.

God's Cop tied a much-mocked religious populist (and local chief constable), to the scally life of drugs, money, sex and more drugs as, with trademark bravado, Shaun tells us "me 'n' the chief got slowly stoned". Donovan opens with cocktail-lounge Latin rhythms before it mutates into a tribute to the Sixties Dylan-wannabe responsible for the gentle Sunshine Superman. Where Donovan's trip was a voyage of wonder, the Mondays' version recounted yet another misspent, loved-up afternoon of bad behaviour, which still sounds most appealing. Part of the Mondays' appeal comes from this ability to make the bizarre seem desirable; in Grandbag's Funeral for example, the twisted guitars and bent-up Talking Heads-style funk introduce a story of getting totally messed up at a serious family occasion.

Dennis And Lois is a rose-tinted look back to the band's innocent youth-club days. A carefree tale of fighting, screwing and taking drugs, it segues neatly into the bedroom nasty of Bob's Your Uncle, a sleazy groove with lyrics that sound like Eric Burdon leafing through Ryder's dirty movie collection; "four in a bed, three getting wet, one giving head".

Step On, a rousing, ecstatic strut, turns John Kongos' Seventies protest song into a party anthem. Of the final two linked tracks, Holiday is a scally smuggling story of baggage and body searches ("You don't look first class, let me look up your ass") and run-ins with the customs, while Harmony is musical confirmation of the feeling that comes from getting through with the packages undiscovered; bliss, relief, thanks and joy. A beautiful chill-out closer, it features subliminal vocals and a little elegant guitar feedback, while tipping a cheeky hat to the New Seekers' "I'd Like To Teach The World To Sing".

➲ We almost chose **Bummed**, London, 1988

# 36

# Jimi Hendrix Experience

## Are You Experienced

MCA, 1967; reissued with bonus tracks MCA, 1997

Jimi Hendrix (gtr, vocals), Noel Redding (bass, gtr, vocals), Mitch Mitchell (drums), Lonnie Youngblood (sax, vocals).

When **Are You Experienced** was released in 1967, Jimi Hendrix seemed to have sprung fully fledged from the collective fantasies of the English acid scene, but he had in fact served a long musical apprenticeship. After several years paying his dues on the American "chitlin" r'n'b circuit, touring with the Isley Brothers and Little Richard among others, he went solo in 1966, playing small gigs in New York City. Success only came when he was brought to England by Chas Chandler (formerly bass player with the Animals) and Mike Jeffrey (the Animals' manager). Hooking up with Redding and Mitchell as the Jimi Hendrix Experience, he was soon burning up a storm first in the clubs of London, and then across the UK. Hendrix introduced a black psychedelic rock style to British audiences already familiar with black soul, jazz and bluebeat singers. In many ways, for all their fearsome noise, the Experience resembled a tight jazz trio more than a conventional rock band, with the different instruments sharing the limelight and communicating with an almost telepathic understanding.

From the first moment of Foxy Lady – where the guitar swoops overhead to home in like some electric predator – there's a sense of immense power barely held in check. Even during quieter songs, like May This Be Love, the lower volume merely allows more of the technical wizardry to show through.

"Foxy Lady" blends an unforgettable riff, horny lyrics and swaggering vocal delivery with sleek, glistening, guitar solos, while Manic Depression, which follows, features another solo that leaves the competition coughing in the dust. Further techno-flash peaks are conquered during Red House, a Hendrix composition that recalls the classic electric blues of the Forties and Fifties. Starting out with a blistering solo run, it's adorned with unbelievable frills played after each line of lyrics, from sustained three-note wails to blinding squalls at unquantifiable speed.

Amid a sustained sequence of tracks that have become staples of rock radio, it's still possible to pick out flashes of transcendent magic, such as the solo perched on the brink of uncontrolled feedback during the bravura posturing of Can You See Me, the acidic space-groove of Love Or Confusion and Third Stone From The Sun (whose riff was borrowed by Right Said Fred for "I'm Too Sexy"), or the trippy interplay of music and Hendrix's lost voice in I Don't Live Today. Studio effects do nothing to dull the brilliance of the music; the production comes into its own in the deeply tranquillized "May This Be Love", where percussion takes the lead role.

Bonus tracks on the CD re-release include epic early singles like Hey Joe and the latin-tinged Stone Free – a macho "talkin' bout my generation" for the hippy head – as well as the jazz-rocky 51st Anniversary, one of the all-time great anti-marriage songs, and the unforgettable rocking stomp of Purple Haze, one of the all-time great pro-acid songs.

Hendrix shone briefly but intensely bright, re-defining all previous notions of the electric guitar, and creating as enduring an influence as the Beatles but taking only three years to do so. The profound admiration he won from his peers in both jazz and contemporary music, and his ongoing reputation as *the* guitarist to match, make *Are You Experienced* – his purest and strongest work – one of the most important rock records ever. More than thirty years down the line, it still takes the breath away.

➲ We almost chose Axis: **Bold As Love**, Track, 1968

# 37

# Hole

## Live Through This

Geffen, 1994

Courtney Love (gtr, vocals), Eric Erlandson (gtr), Kristen Pfaff (bass, pno, vocals),
Patty Schemel (drums), Dana Kletter (vocals).

Consistently loud, defiantly spoiled-brattish, and fully in the media's face for the last decade, Hole have never ceased to sneer, nor once hesitated to kick ass. The bulk of the credit belongs to one of the toughest women in rock, Courtney Love, who following brief stints in Faith No More and Babes In Toyland was in Seattle by 1990, looking to form a band of her own. Having recruited Erlandson through a want-ad, she hooked up with an all-girl rhythm section, and put out an EP and a single, burning up the local clubs at the same time. Hole made their full-length debut in 1991 with *Pretty On The Inside*, produced by Kim Gordon of Sonic Youth – still one of the loudest pieces of sand-blasting, paint-stripping rock ever recorded – and picked up good press on both sides of the Atlantic for their take-no-prisoners style.

Through 1992 and most of 1993, the band was put on hold while Love and Kurt Cobain got together, had a baby, did heroin and whipped up a storm of scandal. They then returned, totally revamped – only Love and Erlandson remained from the debut – to record **Live Through This**.

The album was a triumphant, masterful combination of Love's unique voice, poetic phrasing, powerchord riffing and intense imagery, with Erlandson's sweeter melodies and more delicate touch. Although the new line-up brought Hole's sound closer to that of Nirvana, it was undeniably Love's vision that defined the band; she wrote the songs, and they reflected her concerns. Love was the clever feminist in Doll Parts and Miss World, both of which bristled with her trademark rage and troop-rallying rhetoric, and she shuddered with pain, leaning heavily on the band for support, through I Think That I Would Die and She Walks On Me. The band's brooding anger bubbles through Plump and Asking For It, riffs growing chunkier, drums more insistent, the lyrics emphasized by the classy major-label production, but the songs are strong enough in themselves to shatter the crystalline clarity and let the sheer, untouched emotional energy blaze through. There's genuine bitterness behind the hard-edged pop of Gutless and a harsh, unfettered pessimism to Rock Star that's hard to fake.

The growing humanity in Love's songwriting was brought into raw, poignant focus in Jennifer's Body, with lyrics that coincidentally point to Cobain's forthcoming suicide ("With a bullet, number one / Kill the family, save the son").

Just days before *Live Through This* was due for release, in April 1994, Cobain killed himself, and the album disappeared in the worldwide media flurry. Two months later, bassist Pfaff died as the result of an overdose, to be replaced by Melissa Auf Der Maur. Another two-month delay ensued before Love and the band were finally in shape to tour, and the momentum had been lost. Though *Live Through This* eventually went gold and topped critics' polls in the *New York Times*, *Village Voice* and *Rolling Stone*, Hole, thanks to the notoriety of their lead singer, were fated to remain in Nirvana's shadow. Despite constant touring and their 1998 album *Celebrity Skin*, they have never really broken free of Cobain's influence. Even so, despite being picked up and discarded by both the Riot Grrrl and indie/alt.rock crowds, Hole have stomped onward through tragedy and critical adversity, never wavering in their more-louder-faster mission. Thanks to Love's psychotic-baby-doll pose, angry kids with attitude now have a female role model to look up to.

➲ We almost chose **Celebrity Skin**, Geffen, 1998

# 38

# Hüsker Dü

## New Day Rising

SST, 1985

Bob Mould (gtr, bass, pcn, pno, vocals), Greg Norton (bass, vocals), Grant Hart (pcn, pno, drums, vocals).

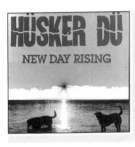

There was a time in the mid-Eighties when Minneapolis, Minnesota – "America's most liveable city" – seemed to rule the world. Prince, The Time, and Jam & Lewis owned urban radio, while The Replacements and Hüsker Dü dominated the rock underground. Heck, even professional wrestling, the biggest passion of a state destined to be governed by Jesse "The Body" Ventura, was experiencing unprecedented popularity. While they never camped up their aggression with make-up and theatricality, Hüsker Dü, like their heroes from the squared circle, harnessed raw power with captivating hooks to create some of the most cathartic music imaginable.

By 1983, hardcore had kicked against all the pricks it possibly could, and Hüsker Dü realized that the only way forward without regressing to metal was to incorporate melody. 1983's *Metal Circus* and 1984's *Zen Arcade* saw the band move away from the purist hardcore of their earlier records, but it was **New Day Rising** that established Hüsker Dü as the finest power trio this side of those other great proponents of umlaut rock, Motörhead.

Despite the implicit optimism of both title and cover, *New Day Rising* is no Bobby McFerrin album. Like all the best pop music, it's all about the exquisite pain of heartbreak. Unless you're feeling generous (in which case Al Green's *Call Me* is what you're after), *New Day Rising* is the best break-up album ever made: pissed off and hurt, but not so dark you can't see the light at the end of the tunnel. On the first two tracks, New Day Rising and Girl Who Lives on Heaven Hill, vocalists Bob Mould and Grant Hart eviscerate their pain like they're escapees from the nearest EST clinic. On the third, I Apologize, Mould lets his guitar do all the primal screaming.

Unlike other post-punk bands with similarly damaged psyches, Hüsker Dü tempered their spleen with admissions of weakness. You won't find queer-bashing or rampant misogyny here – all the self-loathing is on the surface. The combination of inclusive hooks, hints of fragility, macho riffs and emotional baptism by speed is so perfect that it's a wonder that only the Buzzcocks thought of it sooner. The reason, though, that Hüsker Dü are merely one of the greatest rock bands of all time, and not one of the greatest pop bands, is their frightening intensity. Despite the melodic touches, New Day Rising has none of pop's great disguises: no stylization camouflages Mould's bitterness, no artifice sweetens his nasal rasp, no jingle-jangle masks the distortion.

New Day Rising was too naked to achieve commercial success, but there's plenty here that deserved radio play. Books About UFOs might just be the best lonely girl song ever written (and that's saying something), while Celebrated Summer is what Boston's "More Than a Feeling" would sound like if they'd been responding to punk not Led Zeppelin, and Terms of Psychic Warfare ranks as a kiss-off with Bob Dylan's "Positively Fourth Street". Then again, the guitar squall of Plans I Make must have scared the crap out of Slayer's Kerry King, and Whatcha Drinkin' and I Don't Know What You're Talking About are thrashy tantrums set to music. Whatever your predilection, only the dissonance of How to Skin a Cat ever drags.

While Superchunk and Soul Asylum tried to pick up Hüsker Dü's power-pop mantle, New Day Rising and the just-as-good follow-up, Flip Your Wig, marked the last time Amerindie rock truly engaged with punk. After this, it was all Seattle sludge and bands unsuccessfully observing the (Black) Sabbath.

➲ We almost chose **Warehouse: Songs and Stories**, Warner, 1987

# 39

# Jane's Addiction

## Nothing's Shocking

Warner, 1988

Perry Farrell (vocals), Dave Navarro (gtr), Eric A (bass), Stephen Perkins (pcn).

One of the great shamans of the art-rock scene, Perry Farrell surrounded himself with the disturbed cream of Los Angeles' alt.rock misfits to form Jane's Addiction in 1987. On the strength of their self-titled live debut album, they stormed out of the LA clubs to become the thinking kids' band of choice by the end of the Eighties, generating a terrifying, captivating, pure rock alternative to their big-haired, posturing metal contemporaries.

**Nothing's Shocking** brought a new corrosive menace to the party, a sense of first-hand acquaintance with genuine evil, with a production job that made everything sound louder than everything else, while Farrell just kept on straining and spitting even during the quieter sections. Farrell's extensive background reading in black magic, coupled with Navarro's taste for colossal powerchords, helped to build a reputation for mind-corrupting, drug-fuelled music, stained with blood and other, less wholesome bodily fluids. From the cover photograph – not merely a sculpture of two naked women, it had to be two apparently conjoined twins whose heads were in flames – to the deranged handwriting on the reverse, it's an album of stunning confidence and disdain for convention.

*Nothing's Shocking* opens with the relative restraint of Up The Beach – sub-Led Zeppelin drone, epic golden-age guitar soloing and a mere five words on the lyric sheet ("Here we go now, home"). Then the real stuff is unleashed, in Ocean Size, whose deceptively gentle introduction unfolds into a monstrous power-riffing beast, sparkling with echoed vocal and a searing solo. The music swells and retreats like a tidal river before it rounds off with a nice arty touch, a false ending. The brooding metalwork continues in Mountain Song – all weighty bass and bucket-loads of guitar, a guaranteed mosh-pit crowd-pleaser – and the heavy-metal philosophy of Pig's In Zen.

On the white metal-funk workout of Had A Dad, the guitar heroics, grinding unstoppable riff and self-conscious lyrics combine to take a good shot at the tricky subjects of parental abandonment and loss of faith. The funk returns in the weirdness of Standing In The Shower, with its strange singalong chorus, and again on the non-conformist battle-hymn Idiots Rule.

The prime cut on *Nothing's Shocking*, and the one from which the title is taken, is Ted, Just Admit It. A slow-building, incandescent challenge to serial killer Ted Bundy to confess his guilt, it's a harrowing collage of Bundy's sampled voice, ominous bass and slow-paced drumming that explodes into the blood-chilling refrain of "sex is violent". Stretching over seven minutes, with its powerful, almost-jazzy, riffed-up finale, it demands comparisons with the Rolling Stones' "Midnight Rambler".

Summertime Rolls lightens the procedings with its happy, marijuana-scented girl/boy theme, swelling cymbals and distant guitar lines. As close as the album comes to a love song, it has a sly humour, growing, from a lone bass run, into a big production before dwindling back to solo bass. Jane Says, the quietest cut, relies on acoustic guitar and mellow steel drum to create a suitable groove to back the strained vocals, and Jane's unreliable-junkie promise, "I'm gonna kick tomorrow".

Jane's Addiction were ridden by demons, documenting night-mare situations with the music of impending doom. Their superb technical skills and total lack of restraint made this one of the most important and, despite the title, most shocking albums of the Eighties.

⮑ We almost chose **Ritual de lo Habitual**, Warner, 1990

# The Jesus And Mary Chain

## Psychocandy

Blanco Y Negro / Warner, 1985

Jim Reid (vocals, gtr), William Reid (gtr, vocals), Douglas Hart (bass), Bobby
Gillespie (drums).

A howling, dangerous amalgam of
feedback, booming vocals and a
drum sound from Phil Spector's
scrapbook, the Jesus and Mary
Chain were described by Creation
Records boss Alan McGee as
"either the best or the worst band
I'd ever seen". Their music had a
greater depth and complexity
than either the teen epics of
Spector or the cartoon fun of the
Ramones with which it was most often compared, while the
sparse lyrics aimed at generating feelings rather than simply
telling tales. Jim's stoned-sounding vocals matched those of Ian
Brown (Stone Roses) for detached cool, and William's guitar,
fuzzed beyond legal limits, gave them a solid wall off which to
echo. Bobby Gillespie, perhaps realizing that he'd need to master
more than the opening to "Be My Baby" if he was to make it as
a rock drummer, had already formed Primal Scream, but contributed just the restrained, distant mortar-shell percussion that
was needed to lend structure to the sonic assault. Together they
assembled a cynical and resigned pop music that was perfect for
the disaffected kids of the mid-Eighties, and was unveiled, fully
formed, on their debut album, **Psychocandy**.

Introductions to songs, where they exist at all, are limited to
one or two drum breaks. In general, a wall of guitar force and
reverberating voice suddenly explodes, and the song is under
way. With most tracks coming in at under three minutes, brevity,

and a generous helping of distorted six-string noise, is all. Thus Taste Of Cindy – a Velvet Underground-style driving guitar groove distilled to the length of a Ramones track – clocks in at a mere one minute forty seconds. Even the longest track, You Trip Me Up – also released as a single – extends to four minutes only by relying on a protracted instrumental coda.

Another earlier single release, Just Like Honey, kicks things off. Shimmering, echoey vocals and restrained – though still reassuringly fuzzed-up – guitars mix sweetly with Ronettes-style backing vocals in the album's most ornately orchestrated moment. It shares its mood of "relationship's end" melancholy with The Hardest Walk, a fuzz-guitar tribute to the Beach Boys' "Cut Dead" that's also an overt homage to the Righteous Brothers, and Sowing Seeds, a coolly cruising search for peace.

The distorted six-string mechanics get an even greater chance to shine on faster, rockier cuts like The Living End. Dealing with speed, leather, motorcycles, sex and death, with all the drive of Hawkwind's riffs-for-crossing-galaxies, the song looks back to Suicide's 1977 motorbike-rebel anthem "Johnny". In A Hole starts with blaring dentists'-drill feedback and pounding go-to-hell drums to back its lyrics of doom (such as "God spits on my soul"), then unbelievably succeds in cranking up the intensity for the finale. Some Candy Talking turns from a wall-of-sound opus to a sordid druggy groove (much like the Velvets' "Waiting For The Man"), while Never Understand takes surf music to drugged-up extremes, lashed in gales of feedback.

The Mary Chain project reaches its limits on Take The Floor, where the guitars sound like a clenched fistful of razor blades; It's So Hard, with its mighty, march-paced drums; and My Little Underground, a feast of reverb that was apparently recorded in a tunnel. Their "wall of force" sounds every bit as mean and risky at the end of the Nineties as it did on release. Dark, lonely and drug-addled, *Psychocandy* is a sombre masterpiece of Eighties rock.

⮑ We almost chose **Darklands**, Blanco Y Negro, 1987

# 41

# Joy Division

## Unknown Pleasures

Factory, 1979

Bernard Albrecht (gtr, kbds), Ian Curtis (vocals), Peter Hook (bass), Stephen Morris (drums).

Joy Division's bleak, unremitting gaze at the urban wastelands of late Seventies Manchester introduced an even darker tinge to the "no-future" manifesto of British punk. The ten uniformly doom-struck tracks of their official debut album, **Unknown Pleasures**, catalogue depression, regret and impulsive action on the brink of a second dark age, all laid over music that's characterized by purposefully soulless electronic bleeps, guitars swathed in studio trickery, and urgent driving percussion. In a Manchester echo of the citified paranoia of Pere Ubu, Joy Division created a "psyche-traumatic" music ideally suited to the times.

Opening with Can-inspired "motorik" drumming, bass deployed as lead instrument, and spooky whooshes of echoing, edgy guitar, Disorder, the first track, lays out the 256 shades of grey in Joy Division's palette. Martin Hannet's empty-sounding production cushions Ian Curtis' sepulchral voice as it tells of waiting for a guide to come and take him by the hand – a theme of helplessness that was constantly to recur.

The thoughtfully paced single-string guitar runs that punctuate the gloom; the half-heard apologies and whispered regrets; the frenzied synthesizer bursts; the clanging locks and gates; all combine to document nights spent in bitter drug-fuelled argument. Curtis' cries of despair and resignation are delivered with a harrowing sincerity. His lyrical descent into the comforts of madness seems not merely understandable but positively seductive.

New Dawn Fades continues this oblique feeling of failure, transporting it to an "end of the affair" setting. A disjointed, squawking and hesitant introduction introduces a slow, pregnant bassline and ominous Mick Ronson-style guitar chops. Curtis' speaking voice was reedy and high-pitched, but for singing, and for this piece in particular, he drew on the spirit of Scott Walker to ignite torch-song melodramatics. When he lets his emotions loose on lines such as "I walked on water, ran through fire", it is simply impossible to remain unmoved.

The echoing drums and restrained buzzsaw guitar sounds of Wilderness stress impotence and frustration at a merciless series of visions of disaster, moving into the rocker from Hell that is Interzone, which draws both title and inspiration from William Burroughs' city of a million backstreet shady deals. An urban night-time march, with fists and teeth tight-clenched, it's a shaky, nervous scurry across town to score more drugs when, frankly, more than enough has already been taken.

The album shudders to a halt with I Remember Nothing, a chilling account of a domestic dispute seen from the dispassionate point of view of one of the emotionally drained parties involved. As the song moves forward, attraction almost becomes love before it sours, giving way to hatred and anger. Apologies for being "away too long" and "me in my own world"; shame, after "violent, more violent, his hand cracks the chair"; and the bitter, wrenching regret of "trapped in a cage and surrendered too soon" combine to depict a marriage turned to loathing, apparently based on Curtis' own chaotic relationship with his wife.

A purgative, cleansing album, despite its unremitting negativity, *Unknown Pleasures* leaves the listener desperate for familiar, friendly human contact.

➲ We almost chose **Still**, Factory, 1981

# 42

# King Crimson

## In The Court Of The Crimson King

EG, 1969; remastered by Robert Fripp, EG, 1989

Robert Fripp (gtr), Ian McDonald (reeds, woodwinds, kbds), Greg Lake (bass, vocals), Michael Giles (drums, pcn), Peter Sinfield (words and illumination).

In its early days, progressive rock could be as sharp as a knife, and cut to the quick just as easily. Before its admittedly magnificent pomp – bloated with ever more bizarre percussion instruments, precarious banks of keyboards, multi-necked guitars and weapons-grade light shows – prog-rock packaged its overblown sagas of warlocks and warlords within a technically impeccable, complex new rock format that demanded previously unheard-of levels of skill and dexterity. The introduction of a jazz-like emphasis on instrumental prowess was to lead to the deification of guitar "gods" simply in terms of how many notes they could play per second, but at this stage it remained more important to know which notes to play. Characterized above all by its sheer, glowing intelligence and the unparalleled art of the players, the music of King Crimson drew on elements that ranged from free jazz to hippy-style acoustic folk, and exploited dynamic light and shade by means of techniques adopted from the classical orchestra.

As the Sixties gave way to the Seventies, **In The Court Of The Crimson King** set new standards for rock, displaying a new, paranoid, electric vision whose tension was lifted only sporadically by quieter acoustic interludes. Remastered for CD by Robert Fripp, the country's most innovative guitarist, it gained in clarity, to become as stripped-down and cruel as a hatchet man from head office; a relic from the days of nineteen-word song titles, shining with bitter purity.

The cataclysmic opening track, 21st Century Schizoid Man, lays out the agenda with awesome conviction and power. Fierce distorted vocals, driven home by jabbing keyboards, yell stark lyrics of collapse and destruction. The lengthy mid-section, subtitled "Mirrors", is a high-speed jazz-rocker that features messed-up guitar noises, excellent soloing, and intricate stop-start rhythms, before the strident, noise-filled finale.

The contrast with I Talk To The Wind, which follows, could not be greater. That stoned self-scrutiny, aflutter with the gentle woodwind tones of British psychedelia, is matched by the regretful lullaby of Moonchild, with its two subsections. One is a precursor of the ambient sound sculpture of the Nineties, all shimmering keyboards and quiet traces of guitar, the other an exploration of inner space fuelled by looped guitar runs and punctuated by hints of percussion like rain against a window.

Epitaph showcases the album's third major trademark; layers of swirling, melancholic Mellotron behind ominously impenetrable lyrics. At times perilously close to Moody Blues territory, it's rescued by the duelling of acoustic guitar and keyboard.

As befits its epic, "big production number" status, The Court Of The Crimson King is saved till last. Again divided into subsections ("The Return of the Fire Witch" and "The Dance of the Puppets"), it stalks from grinding, imperious power riffs to soaring, close-harmonied vocals, the lyrics dripping with "purple pipers" and "the rusted chain of prison moons", an overblown vocabulary employed in a brave attempt to build a new mythology for a blissed-out audience of older children. The stunning instrumentals, humour and contrasting moods combine to create an unforgettable expression of late Sixties genius.

From the apocalyptic opening, through Greg Lake's pastoral acoustic soundscapes, to the room-shaking powerchords with which it closes, *In The Court Of The Crimson King* highlights the mighty force of progressive rock when it truly was progressive.

➲ We almost chose **Thrak**, Virgin, 1995

# Kraftwerk

## Trans-Europe Express

Capitol, 1977

Ralf Hutter (vocals, kbds, drums), Florian Schneider (vocals, kbds, drums), Wolfgang Flur (pcn, synths), Karl Bartos (pcn).

1977 was *the* year for synthesizer records. Donna Summer, Giorgio Moroder and Pete Bellotte created the icy, mechano-erotic masterpiece "I Feel Love", while Parliament used the Moog to generate the greatest bassline of all time on "Flashlight". Kraftwerk's **Trans-Europe Express**, though, was even more important. It would not be an overstatement to say that Kraftwerk are the most important band of the last quarter of a century, and *Trans-Europe Express* was their meisterwork.

Pop has always been the realm of stylization and artifice, but its obsession with sheen and plasticity can be traced to Kraftwerk. Ralf Hutter and Florian Schneider's early albums – recorded with Klaus Dinger and Michael Rother, who went on to form the "motorik" masters Neu! – were largely chimescapes with an undertow of Velvet Underground propulsion. By the time of *Trans-Europe Express*, however, the band had sprinkled their pristine surfaces with enough spangle to influence a generation of Bowie-fixated, glamour-infatuated British mannequin boys to ditch their guitars in favour of Korgs, Yamahas and Rolands.

Meanwhile in New York, exploiting the surreal popularity enjoyed by Düsseldorf's showroom dummies in the discos and block parties, Afrika Bambaata, keyboardist John Robie and producer Arthur Baker welded the melody of Trans-Europe Express onto the synth-bass of Computer World's "Numbers" and the percussion from Captain Sky's "Super Sperm" to create "Planet Rock" – the Rosetta Stone of electro, and the song that taught the world that machines were just as funky as James Brown. While Kraftwerk would never even break a sweat, dance genres like techno and Miami Bass would be unthinkable without their pioneering explorations of the synthesized netherworld.

Kraftwerk helped to make the world safe for both Aphex Twin and Steps, and their own music was riddled with this same tension between pop and experiment. A love of surface and pure sound, coupled with a prescient embrace of the aesthetic of flux, meant that their music glistened as much as it bleeped. Like their fellow travellers, Japan's Yellow Magic Orchestra, Kraftwerk used electronics to rebaptize postwar German culture. An entangled web of parody and camp, *Trans-Europe Express* celebrated speed, purity, German efficiency and a united Europe with enough vacant showbiz glitz to make Busby Berkeley blush. It was all so deadpan that you had to wonder whether they were serious.

The music offers few clues. The synthscapes of Showroom Dummies and The Hall of Mirrors are gloomy death marches perfectly matched to tales of alienation. On the other hand, Europe Endless sees Kraftwerk at their most majestic – all shimmering tinkles and whooshing synth surges – while Franz Schubert is exactly the delirious meeting of electronics and classical music the title would lead you to hope.

The highlight here, though, is the suite of "Trans-Europe Express" and Metal on Metal. Everything the Italian Futurists wanted to be but never were, the Doppler-effect synth swishes and "chhh-ch-ch-ch-chhh" rhythms create a delicious parody of locomotion. While on the surface the songs are glorious odes to velocity and the new world order, the ludicrously camp name-dropping lyrics ("From station to station back to Düsseldorf city / To meet Iggy Pop and David Bowie") undercut the vision of a man-machine utopia to create an ambivalence that's even more profound for not taking itself too seriously.

⮑ We almost chose **Autobahn**, EMI, 1974

# 44

# Led Zeppelin

## Led Zeppelin III

Atlantic, 1970

Jimmy Page (gtr), Robert Plant (harp, vocals), John Paul Jones (bass, kbds), John Bonham (drums).

A sledgehammer riff, a testosterone-fuelled wail from the other side of Valhalla, and a bludgeoning drum pattern that threatens permanent damage to the speakers – and that's just the first few seconds. Yet Led Zeppelin were always far too large to fit in the heavy rock pigeonhole, and their third album encapsulates the mix of influences that enabled them to transcend categorization. These strands include English folk, Mississippi blues, and Indian raga; when stamped with the band's identity and a sharp production, the brew is intoxicating, and explains why Led Zeppelin continue to be the most commercially successful rock band on the planet.

**Led Zeppelin III** was released in 1970 with an elaborate, rotating gatefold sleeve. The previous year the band's groundbreaking first two albums had stormed the charts on both sides of the Atlantic, and incessant touring had consolidated their status as leaders of the rock underground. The follow-up inevitably entered the US and UK charts at number one, toppling the Beatles' *Abbey Road* in the process, but the critics, expecting simply another slab of hard rock in the vein of "Whole Lotta Love", were confused by its diversity. While it does indeed start with the merciless riffarama of Immigrant Song, an uncompromising tale of Viking pillage, that's followed by the dirge-like Friends, heavily influenced by Indian musical structures.

Celebration Day and Out On The Tiles are more standard rock fare, but the simmering blues of Since I've Been Loving You slows things down once again, as Page launches into one of the most passionate solos of his career. Plant doesn't so much sing the song as use his voice as an instrument of tortured dementia.

Most of what was side two is acoustic, having been conceived at Bron-Y-Aur, a remote cottage in Snowdonia which the band had rented for pastoral inspiration; exhausted from touring, it was time, according to Plant, "to step back, take stock and not get too lost in it all." Gallow's Pole is a traditional folk tune adapted from a version by Leadbelly, which builds into a frenzied jig of swirling banjo, mandolin and electric bass, while the reflective Tangerine dates back to Page's stint with the Yardbirds. That's The Way, a story of starcrossed lovers that's replete with images of generational discord and ecological concerns ("All the fish that lay in dirty water, dying / Had they got you hypnotized?"), boasts some of Plant's finest lyrics and some deft pedal-steel guitar.

Bron-Y-Aur Stomp, a lighthearted jugband shuffle embellished by particularly nimble picking, leads into the final track, Hats Off To (Roy) Harper. Zeppelin only recorded a couple of turkeys in their entire career, but this tribute to the longstanding stalwart of the British folk scene is one of them. Despite the rootsy bottleneck guitar (modelled on Bukka White), Plant's vocals are treated to sound as if he's singing on Radio Caroline on a stormy night. It's hard to imagine why the track was included at the expense of the ebullient "Hey Hey What Can I Do" (now available on *Remasters*), which must rate as one of the band's best folk-rock compositions.

That said, *Led Zeppelin III* showed that rock could progress by drawing on the past, and that what might seem a superficial, magpie approach to world music could still result in an intimate and enduring experience. And, turned up full blast, it could still drive the neighbours crazy.

⮑ We almost chose **Led Zeppelin II**, Atlantic, 1969

# 45

# Leftfield

## Leftism

Hard Hands/Sony, 1995

Paul Daley (kbds), Neil Barnes (kbds).

Leftfield were an underground success responsible for introducing a punk-ish, dub-informed sensibility to the London dance scene. Their rich and juicy list of influences enabled them to please diehard clubbers while getting in touch with conventional rock and indie audiences. Like the Orb, Chemical Brothers and Orbital, they employed a familiar musical vocabulary to communicate their dance-based work to first-timers, and their vision soon proved entirely capable of expanding to fill an album-length recording, **Leftism**.

Although Leftfield's singles had been attracting attention since 1990, not until they signed to Hard Hands in 1992 did they begin to reach a dramatically wider audience. Release The Pressure and Song Of Life (both included here) moved out of the clubs onto network radio, but it was the masterful choice of the unmistakable John Lydon as guest vocalist on 1993's Open Up that took them from clubland to number twenty in the singles charts, and thence to the sitting rooms of the world.

The whole point of *Leftism* was to extract Leftfield from the underground, and it did so immensely well. Much of *Leftism* works like an instruction manual on how to make dance music, with quiet, slowly paced, spacey introductions that swell to become irresistible floor-fillers. The classic Leftfield technique is to build a mix, adding components one at a time, pause for a while to admire the complex beauty of the entire edifice, and then carefully strip away the instruments one by one until only the skeleton remains. Thus bubbling keyboard sounds blend with "rainforest" animal noises, or Hugh Masakela trumpet-frills are painstakingly re-created on a synthesizer.

There's also an invigorating infusion of guest vocalists. African rapper Djum Djum worked with Kevin Haynes's berimbou (a strung percussion instrument that hums like a buzzing fly caught in a harmonium) on Afro-Left, while reggae singers Earl Sixteen and Papa Dee paired up with legendary engineer Joe Gibbs for "Release The Pressure", and Curve's Toni Halliday supplied haunting vocals for Original, giving a human face to the maelstrom of electronic effects.

Song Of Life pulls all the influences together, opening with booming bass and ethereal vocal samples before it mutates into a breathy bump'n'grind rhythm that's shadowed by portentous, almost churchy, organ sounds. On Ritual, celebratory wails introduce a double-speed clubland killer dance anthem pumped up by squelching acid keyboards and kicking drums to a full seven minutes. Open Up, a swirl of beats and keyboards topped by Lydon's caustic caterwauling, and 21st Century Poem, a despairing ode by Manchester bard Lemn Sissay that's accompanied by exotic percussive effects and a shimmering wave of constantly changing keyboard sounds, round things off. Bleak images of apocalypse, perhaps, but Lydon is laughing in the teeth of disaster and dancing on the graves of movie stars. There's nothing downbeat about it in the slightest.

Using every corny club-DJ move in the book, Leftfield tease and build tension as they create dance music by numbers: easy to follow, four to the floor, stomping beats with traces of reggae, African-tinged "world" music and soul, plus a dash of rock to help it cross over. That's not to deny their originality, wit or unique personal stamp; a powerful presence on the "progressive house" scene, they have the taste and intelligence to see beyond the beat. and allow the beauty of the music to shine out.

> To date, there's only been one Leftfield album

# 46

# John Lennon / Plastic Ono Band

## John Lennon / Plastic Ono Band

Apple, 1970

John Lennon (gtr, pno, kbds, vocals), Billy Preston (pno, kbds), Ringo Starr (drums), Yoko Ono (vocals, wind, woodwind), Phil Spector (pno), Klaus Voormann (bass).

Attempts to convey deep emotion can all too often appear twee and naive to the cold gaze of the cynical rock audience. The only way through is absolute and transparent sincerity, following the route blazed by **John Lennon / Plastic Ono Band**. Even Lennon himself never managed to equal the album, the most sensitive and moving work by any of the ex-Beatles, in the decade that remained before his death.

In the aftermath of McCartney's announcement that he was leaving the Beatles, the distraught Lennon departed, with his wife Yoko Ono, for Los Angeles. There he subjected himself to intense, draining sessions of Arthur Janov's primal therapy. For the recording that soon followed, Lennon understandably surrounded himself with a band made up of friendly and familiar faces. Ringo Starr, solid as ever, played drums; Klaus Voormann, an old face from the early days in Hamburg (who'd also designed the cover for *Revolver*), took the bass; Yoko supplied the "wind"; and Malcolm Evans (old hand at the Apple organization) provided tea and sympathy. Phil Spector contributed an unusually light touch to the production, double-tracking Lennon's voice throughout and establishing his trademark solo-era vocal sound, but otherwise staying firmly out of the spotlight. The convivial surroundings, however, did little to lift the unremittingly sombre mood. It might not seem wise to go through such traumas in public, but Lennon, who had spent most of his adult life in the studio, was never likely to do otherwise.

Mother opens with the distorted tolling of a funeral bell, immediately echoed by a sustained, insistent piano chord, and we are introduced to the first and greatest of the demons Lennon confronted during therapy – his mother Julia, who handed him over to his aunt as a child, and died when John was seventeen. With lyrics that verge at times on the oedipal and a voice on the brink of sobs, it's a stark blues in which Lennon also addresses his absent father, who deserted the family soon after his birth. The laid-back riff of Hold On masks the raw pain of Lennon's struggle to stay sober, highlighting the priceless support offered by Yoko – who had a few demons of her own to stare down.

The all-pervasive sense of bitterness, however, is at its most evident in the searing solo rendition of Working Class Hero. A folk-song catalogue of life's iniquities, it showcases Lennon's strongest vocal performance, as considered as anything he'd recorded with the Beatles. On Well, Well, Well, it's the turn of the angry Lennon, determined both to stay mad and to get even, to step to the microphone. The list of worthy causes, tinged with liberal guilt, appears dated now, but offers an illuminating insight into the pressures of playing the working-class hero, plus an eloquent, jagged guitar break that takes over when words fail him.

The superficial arrogance of Look At Me vanishes once the self-doubt and affection of the lyrics becomes apparent, but God, despite its sugary arrangement (with an intro taken almost note for note from "Love Letters Straight From The Heart", and piano courtesy of Billy Preston), maintains a consistent negative feel, as Lennon catalogues his hatreds, until the final moments.

The confessional mood remains for the intriguing closing track, My Mummy's Dead, on which Lennon's distorted voice chants a nursery-rhyme lyric – echoing the rhythms of "Three Blind Mice" – over what sounds like a toy guitar. The harrowing doggerel of the lyrics sees the album's initial anger turned to sadness and regret, his lost mother finally laid to rest.

➲ We almost chose **Imagine**, EMI/Geffen, 1971

# 47

# Little Richard

## 22 Classic Cuts

Ace, 1986

Little Richard (vocals, pno), Earl Palmer (drums), Lee Allen (sax), Alvin Tyler (sax).

For his sheer, kick-the-doors-in piano-playing attitude, for his flamboyance, his perspiration-drenched pompadour hairdo, and the godlike genius of his "Whooo!", Little Richard Penniman deserves his place in rock'n'roll history. Each of the dozens of greatest hits collections on the market will boast some of the tracks featured here, but **22 Classic Cuts** stands out as the only complete document of Little Richard during his years on the Specialty label. It contains all his everlasting classics, from Long Tall Sally, which charted in 1956, through to his camp take on Baby Face (1958), and By The Light Of The Silvery Moon (1959).

Rock'n'roll was already kicking off, and Little Richard was already an experienced crowd-destroying musician, by the time he sat down to record in New Orleans in 1955. Elvis was busting out of his hillbilly niche, Chuck Berry was chasing "Maybellene" all over the country, but Little Richard had been on the road since he was thirteen, and was every bit as ready for success.

His stage act borrowed ideas from Billy Wright (the makeup-wearing, fluorescently-dressed bluesman who'd introduced Penniman to RCA records earlier in the decade), while he'd picked up some piano tips from Esquerita (who'd known Richard Penniman back when he was plain old Princess Lavonne in a red sequinned gown), but he was an undeniable original, as he himself declared: "King Of The Blues, and The Queen too".

Although Specialty had originally planned to market Little Richard as a straightforward blues or gospel artist, the barnstorming Tutti Frutti (which Richard had been busking with the band during a break in the session) was chosen as his first release for the label. One of the staff writers, Ms Dorothy LaBostrie, was responsible for cleaning up the possibly illegal and definitely salacious "tight booty" lyric to the equally rock'n'roll "aw rootie". The single went to number two in the US r'n'b chart, number seventeen in the US pop charts, and was even a top thirty success in the UK.

From then on, as hectic touring schedules were set up to capitalize on the success of that and subsequent singles, recording sessions could only be snatched hastily between dates. Even on lovingly remastered compilations such as this, the band disappears every now and then into the mix, but the essential, pulse-quickening joy of Little Richard's vocal delivery, and the frenetic madness of his piano, cuts through each time.

Thanks to the rampant bigotry of many white-owned US radio stations at the time, much of Little Richard's income was at first generated through plain vanilla cover versions, recorded by such fiercely inappropriate mannequins as Pat Boone (who took "Tutti Frutti" to the number one spot, and also charted with Long Tall Sally), or the more credible Elvis Presley (who also covered "Tutti Frutti" and "Long Tall Sally", and had a fair stab at Rip It Up too). For once, however, justice was to prevail, and Little Richard was soon consistently hitting the charts himself. In 1956, he won a Billboard triple crown for the most popular, most played and most sold records of the year.

In his four years at Specialty he recorded thirteen singles; unforgettable A-sides and surprisingly strong B-sides, most of which, in the manner of the day, were re-positioned when he briefly retired from the music biz in 1957 and charted in their own right. He's been in and out of Christianity, in and out of rock'n'roll, and in and out of trouble ever since, but this album, this is the juice.

➲ We almost chose **The Specialty Box**, Specialty, 1989

# 48

# Love

## Forever Changes

Elektra, 1967

Arthur Lee (gtr, vocals), Bryan MacLean (gtr, vocals), Ken Forssi (bass), Michael Stuart (pcn, drums), John Echols (gtr).

Fronted by the charismatic Arthur Lee, Love were elegantly wasted, in the foppish, harmless way that characterized the early days of the acid era. Though superficially comfortable on the freak bandwagon, with vaguely anti-authoritarian lyrics slipped into songs at random, and songs whose subjects and structures were patently informed by the LSD experience which was then all the rage, they never forgot that "long, dark night of the soul" hours could be the price you paid for an afternoon in the park, rapping with God himself.

**Forever Changes** bears all the hallmarks of a classic psychedelic album: fragmented lyrics, left out of context to aid the exploration of inner space; intense, driving music that suddenly dissolves into stately ballads; querulous, insecure vocals given an added acid shudder by nervy guitar runs and tremulous violins. Even so, despite being co-opted into the legend of the Summer Of Love, it pokes gentle fun at the hippy way of life, and reminds the listener that acid, though immense fun, is just another drug that will never change the world. Much like the cod-psychedelia of the Small Faces', "Itchycoo Park", or Traffic's tongue-in-cheek "Hole In My Shoe", the joke has been hidden in the myth.

Opening with Alone again or, a love song for the deeply stoned, and flowing into the blood-stained lyrics of A house is not a motel, *Forever Changes* is unsettling from the very start.

Lee shows a desperate fear of solitude; the frenetic drumming, apocalyptic words, vicious Stooges-style guitar, and yelping, echoing vocals that end the second track all highlight the not-so-great aspects of the end of a trip – the wildly swinging emotions, feverish analysis of offhand remarks, and glimpses of the light at the outer limits of the universe. Freaks, heads, poseurs and wannabe hippys lapped it up like lentil soup.

To give the band their due, they did their best to convey why people were gobbling sugar cubes, blotting paper and Kool-Aid, before giggling and dancing the day away like kids at the fair. Andmoreagain is a gently psychedelic, groovy kind of love song, while The Daily Planet, which follows, starts out with sound rock'n'roll intentions, a little urban paranoia and all-purpose "druggy" lyrics before it begins to lose its way and collapses in a heap. Somehow the band gets it back together again for a classic Sixties rock instrumental fadeout.

Things turn very early-Pink Floyd for Old Man, with its warbling vocal of no fixed melody and weird medieval arrangement, and Red Telephone, made up of snatches of conversation recorded during another of those fabled trippy sessions of spouting rubbish. The chants with which the latter ends – "They're locking them up today, they're throwing away the key, I wonder who it'll be tomorrow, you or me" – and the eerie vocal effects stating "We are normal and we want our freedom", were cruelly parodied soon after by the Bonzo Dog Doo Dah Band.

*Forever Changes* owes a great deal of its impact to the sensitive, unusual arrangements. Strings are employed throughout to provide stoned, outer-space effects and cinematic orchestral sweeps. The Good Humour Man sounds as if Bacharach and David had been marinaded in LSD for a week, before being let loose with pizzicato violins and cheesy brass. After the Dylan tribute of Bummer in the Summer – all sneering vocals and crystal-meth delivery – it closes with the driving rhythm and melodramatic vocal flourishes of You Set The Scene, a seven-minute epic that leaves the listener as drained as a seven-day weekend.

⮊ We almost chose **Da Capo**, Warner, 1967

# 49

# Madonna

## Like a Prayer

Sire, 1989

Madonna (vocals, synth, producer), Marcos Loya (gtr), Chester Kamen (gtr), Guy Pratt (bass), Randy Jackson (bass), Jeff Porcaro (drums), Andrae Crouch (choir), Patrick Leonard (kbds, producer), Stephen Bray (synth, producer), Prince (producer).

Respect didn't come easy for dance-pop diva Madonna Louise Ciccone. Success did, certainly, along with massive popularity and unparalleled cultural influence, but not respect. One big question loomed amid the hype: Did the music matter? Conclusive proof that it did would not arrive until the very end of the decade, with the 1989 release of **Like a Prayer**, which not only bettered – by a long shot – her first three albums, but was a classic statement of self-empowerment.

The stakes were clear from the first song, the stunning Like a Prayer. Scratchy guitar noise plays, a door slams, and her searching voice declares over the hum of a hushed gospel choir, "Life is a mystery, everyone must stand alone. I hear you call my name, and it feels like home." Perhaps it's the dramatic pause before the word "home", or the tension that she allows to build in the space afterwards, but this was the sign of a new, more thoughtful artist. Not one who had forgotten her past, though, for with the onset of the chorus, the party kicks in, full gear. The fact that she pulls off the ensuing combination of Catholicism, sensuality, and funk calls to mind the best attributes of that other Eighties' hitmeister, Prince, who shows up on Love Song. That duet is, surprisingly, a bit of a mess, but it marks the only false note on an album that alternates between perfect pop confection and powerful balladry.

One such theme is that of womanhood, best exemplified by the massive follow-up hit, the anthemic Express Yourself. The same woman who had cooed that, in this material world, she was indeed a "material girl", was now exhorting her sisters that they didn't need diamond rings, fancy cars and satin sheets, that "second best is never enough, you'll do much better baby on your own." Clearly she was speaking, at least in part, from experience. Her marriage in the mid-Eighties to bad-boy actor Sean Pean had been played out in all the tabloids, from whirlwind courtship to ugly divorce in 1988. "Express Yourself" roars along, courtesy of its horns and rhythm guitars, but more so Madonna's bold singing. Where she was once squeaky, even whiny, here she was full of charge and conviction; whether or not she was playing a role this time, it scarcely mattered.

Perhaps the biggest surprise was what occupied the spaces traditionally reserved for so-called filler. True Blue and Like a Virgin had their high spots, to be sure, but each was littered with songs that made you search out the singles. Here, the only other hit was Cherish, a girlish romp in keeping with the past, but programming the CD might mean missing the elegantly sombre Promise to Try, the almost XTC-esque jauntiness of Dear Jessie, or the trembling majesty of Spanish Eyes. Or even the perverse finale, her own Revolution #9, the recitation of the Catholic prayer, the Act of Contrition, over swirling guitar feedback and tape looping. As ever, she has to have the last laugh.

In any case, Like A Prayer stands as Madonna's greatest triumph. She may quite nearly have bettered herself on 1998's Ray of Light, with its winding title track and its ability to respond to all of the changes in dance and pop music since she first entered the scene (or seemed to leave it for motherhood in the mid-Nineties). She may have produced more singular songs than any on Like a Prayer, like "Vogue," a namecheck of the cool that dominated dancehalls and runways seemingly forever. But in a career of defying public expectation, she never did so as winningly. And for that, we should thank our lucky stars.

⮕ We almost chose **Ray of Light**, Maverick / Warner, 1998

# 50

# Massive Attack

## Blue Lines

Wild Bunch, 1991

Robert Del Naja (vocals), Daddy G. Marshall (vocals), Mushroom Vowles (kbds),
Horace Andy (vocals), Shara Nelson (vocals), Tricky (vocals), Mikey General (vocals).

Capturing and essentially defining the UK soundtrack of the early Nineties, Massive Attack were almost single-handedly responsible for the peculiarly British black-meets-white meshing of influences known as trip-hop. **Blue Lines**, their first album, introduced this laid-back, sloweddown, Anglicized blend of hiphop, reggae and turntable techniques, to a mass audience. Massive Attack created a dance music that was chilled to the extent that it was best simply to sway back and forwards on the spot than attempt anything more complicated; dance music to sit down and listen to, which harked back to the marijuana-scented dub reggae scene of the Seventies.

On the whole, white and black communities in Britain are less segregated or distinct than their counterparts in the US, so British popular music tends to experience a freer interchange of ideas and influences. In particular, away from the industry-dominated, pressure-cooker atmosphere of London, localized movements such as trip-hop, which started out in Bristol, can grow and establish themselves in front of black and white audiences.

During the late Eighties, Bristol's party scene was dominated by the Wild Bunch, a DJ/Soundsystem collective with a reputation for mixing soul, reggae and punk. Its pivotal trio – 3-D, Daddy-G and Mushroom – soon realized that their hybrid music was drawing larger crowds than local live acts, and moved from playing records to recording and releasing them, on their own Wild Bunch label. Turning their backs on the herd-mentality of the rave scene, and the twisted, jazz-influenced, breakbeat madness of the jungle crews, they developed an introspective studio-based sound, driven by beats but with "conscious" (thought-provoking) lyrics, a music for thinking more than for funking.

Although Massive Attack's music was almost entirely constructed from a formidable "riff bank" of samples culled from their own record collections, with added electronically generated sounds, it's nonetheless bursting with humanity. When the band themselves didn't supply the vocals, they turned either to reggae icon and master of lovers-rock angst Horace Andy; smouldering soul diva Shara Nelson; Tony Bryan; or fellow Bristol musician Adrian Thaws, better known as Tricky. *Blue Lines* commands respect and attention throughout, from the crystal-clear production, through the immaculate, cinematic sweep of the songs, to the considered wordplay that's evident, for example, as Tricky swaps rhymes with 3-D in Five Man Army.

The impact of *Blue Lines* stopped the British music business in its tracks. Not for the first time, a new sound had appeared, seemingly from nowhere, and rendered everything else instantly obsolete. On Unfinished Sympathy, the most successful of the three tracks from the album that were released as singles, Nelson's gorgeous swooping voice is layered over a compelling, hypnotic beat and elegantly manicured samples. A song of breathtaking beauty as well as immense drive, it became the top-down, booming car stereo hit of the year. Similarly epic torch-song vocals from Nelson adorn Safe From Harm, distinguished by its defiant declaration of love as protection, and Lately.

Besides laying the groundwork for subsequent solo ventures by both Shara Nelson and Tricky, *Blue Lines* revived Horace Andy's career, introducing his intense, almost paranoid voice to a new generation through One Love, Five Man Army, and the closing cut, Hymn Of The Big Wheel.

⮌ We almost chose **Mezzanine**, Virgin, 1998

# 51

# Minutemen

## Double Nickels On The Dime

SST, 1984

D. Boon (gtr, vocals), George Hurley (drums, vocals), Mike Watt (bass, vocals).

When George Orwell's fateful year finally arrived, Springsteen, Tina Turner, Van Halen and Prince were hitting megastardom, while U2 and R.E.M. were well on their way. Meanwhile, a poetically political punk-funk-jazz trio from Los Angeles unleashed an unassuming, sprawling double record on SST, the Eighties equivalent of Sun in the Fifties. Though the band themselves would be the last to call **Double Nickels on The Dime** a masterwork, the sheer size and heft of the thing meant it spelled out their unique vision in more detail than any of their other recordings. Though this sweet excess made the critics roar with approval, *Double Nickels* turned out to be the band's swansong. Even so, Minutemen spearheaded an underground rock movement in the US that soon saw Big Black, the Replacements, and Meat Puppets crawl into the limelight.

Minutemen started out as a quartet in 1978, one of the many bands drawn from the skinheads then populating the punk clubs of LA. Their earliest songs were chants and blurs, in the spirit of their punk daddies. On "What Makes A Man Start Fires?" and "Buzz Or Howl Under The Influence Of Heat," however, they started to unveil more sophisticated ideas, built around the brief, jazzy guitar solos of the humongous D. Boon, the funky, thumping bass of Mike Watt, and George Hurley's intricate drum fills.

By the time of *Double Nickels on The Dime*, the threesome had perfected their rowdy, friendly, angry, impassioned rock stance, while still keeping the songs down to a standard one- or two-minute length. The sleeve depicts the band members in their cars (the sound of motors started and ended each side of the vinyl release), along with savage Raymond Pettibon cartoons, and a slap at their label-mates ("take that, Huskers!"). Although they called the last part of the album "Chaff", and padded it out with covers of Van Halen, Steely Dan (hilariously out-of-it), and Creedence (lo-fi with crowd noise), it was far from a waste product. Highlights like the shoutalong fan-favourite This Ain't No Picnic, the straight-ahead rocker Untitled Song For Latin America, and the mad, desperate Little Man With A Gun In His Hand rank among their strongest songs, period.

Musically, Minutemen were going everywhere, hitting on a jazz-funk fusion à la James Blood Ulmer (they actually jammed with Ornette bassist Charlie Haden), like a looser, sweatier version of the Gang of Four (It's Expected I'm Gone, Nature Without Man, and Maybe Partying Will Help are dead ringers). At the same time, the lovable lunks let their soft side show with pretty pieces like Cohesion, Take 5, D., and There Ain't Shit On TV Tonight. To add a little breadth, they also threw in swing (The Big Foist and Nothing Indeed), Sir Douglas Quintet Tex-Mex (Corona), James Brown salsa (Love Dance), and even sea-shanty (Themselves).

Lyrically, they could fall into slogans ("Viet Nam", "West Germany") but the song titles themselves were, as they put it, worth a thousand words. How can you deny tunes named The Roar of the Masses Could Be Farts, #1 Hit Song, Do You Want New Wave or Do You Want the Truth?, and Political Song For Michael Jackson To Sing?

Sadly, after Boon died in a car accident a year later, the band called it quits, though Watt maintained the spirit with Firehose and his own solo career. *Double Nickels on The Dime* may be no more definitive than any other Minutemen album, but it's an undeniably moving testament to a band that ended too early, the like of which we see all too seldom.

⮑ We almost chose **3-Way Tie (For Last)**, SST, 1985

# 52

# Joni Mitchell

## The Hissing Of Summer Lawns

Asylum, 1975

Joni Mitchell (vocals, gtr, kbds), James Taylor (gtr, vocals), David Crosby (vocals), Graham Nash (harp, vocals), Larry Carlton (gtr), Robben Ford (gtr), Jeff Baxter (gtr), Vic Feldman (kbds), Joe Sample (kbds), Bud Shank (wind), Wilton Felder (bass), Max Bennett (bass), Chuck Findley (horns), John Guerin (drums), Dale Oehler (strings).

Undeniably one of the most important and influential recording artists of the twentieth century, Joni Mitchell has been breaking moulds for more than three decades. A perennial experimenter and consummate songwriter, she reached her creative peak with *The Hissing of Summer Lawns* in 1975, which set new standards for all those who have followed in her idiosyncratic wake.

Having first picked up the guitar as a child in a Canadian hospital, Joni Mitchell progressed through the folk clubs of Toronto to New York and the UK. She originally established her reputation as a songwriter, thanks to hit cover versions by other artists of songs such as "Woodstock". Mainstream acclaim in her own right arrived in 1970, when "Big Yellow Taxi" climbed the singles charts on both sides of the Atlantic. The album from which it came, *Ladies Of The Canyon*, also performed well, while the deeply personal follow-up, *Blue*, took critical and public reaction to even greater heights.

**The Hissing of Summer Lawns** was preceded in 1974 by the lyrical and melodic delights of *Court and Spark* (from which the diverse and charming cuts "Free Man In Paris", "Help Me" and "Raised On Robbery" all performed respectably as singles).

On returning to the studio, however, Mitchell turned her back on *Court and Spark*'s accomplished, lightweight jazz stylings, looking towards a radically darker, more avant-garde sound to carry her increasingly sophisticated songs. Despite the presence of star performers Crosby, Nash and James Taylor, the crucial factors that make *The Hissing of Summer Lawns* so uniquely atmospheric are the masterful guitar work of Carlton and Ford, the claustrophobic drumming of John Guerin, and the frankly weird vocalizing of Mitchell herself.

Opening with In France They Kiss On Main Street, a comparatively conventional set of scenes, chic, romantic and beautifully delivered, the album veers sharply into the left field with The Jungle Line, a booming, disorienting swirl of Burundi drums and synthesizer that would be echoed during the Eighties by the "world music" experiments of Peter Gabriel, Sting and others.

In an album full of surprising moments of peace and beauty, The Hissing of Summer Lawns itself stands out for the sheer delicacy of Mitchell's singing, which is magnificently shaded by the subtle, spacious, jazz-rock backing. Elsewhere, as in the elegant Harry's House/Centerpiece, or Edith And The Kingpin, the overwhelming complexity of the music, and the sheer dexterity of the musicians in rising to its challenges, is awe-inspiring. Swooping between melancholy desolation and breathtaking joy without the slightest faltering in tone, Shadows and Light and Boho Dance best capture Mitchell's strange and fascinating new musical direction.

*The Hissing of Summer Lawns* was the stunning high point of a remarkable series of introspective, at times uncomfortable, albums, in the course of which Mitchell moved from straightforward, folk-tinged reminiscence and confession – the stock in trade of so many Seventies singer-songwriters – to an engrossing, hypnotic music where an exciting weave of rock and jazz cradled a voice mellowed by experience.

➲ We almost chose **Hejira**, Asylum, 1976

# 53

# Van Morrison

## Astral Weeks

Warner, 1968

Van Morrison (vocals, gtr), Jay Berliner (gtr), Richard Davis (bass), Connie Kay (drums), John Payne (flute, sax), Warren Smith, Jr. (pcn, vibes).

Recorded in 1968 in a single, stupendous 48-hour burst, **Astral Weeks** was a creative explosion of deep, thoughtful music, produced by a true artist who had previously been bound by the constraints of mainstream pop. Van Morrison had been in bands since the age of eleven. Having learned his craft in The Monarchs – a showband he put together with his Belfast schoolfriend George Jones – and refined it as a pop star with the group Them, he'd finally achieved solo recognition with "Brown-Eyed Girl" the previous year.

Like many of his British contemporaries, Van Morrison was profoundly influenced by the psychedelic revolution: Eric Burdon quit growling at schoolgirls and headed off to San Francisco to paint flowers on his face, the Rolling Stones found themselves "2000 Light Years From Home", and Morrison washed up in New York City. There, in *Astral Weeks*, he created a ground-breaking album that drew on country music, blues and jazz, and is still selling steadily more than thirty years on. Worshipped by critics and public alike, it employs a rambling, folk-informed palette to paint a lovingly eloquent portrait of city life, infused with dignity and charm. In conjunction with the heartfelt, playful, wide-eyed lyrics, Morrison's vocal fireworks blossomed into a swirling, jazzy new music; confiding, conversational, and straining with sincerity and passion.

All the album's greatest features are presented in spades on the title track, *Astral Weeks* – seven minutes of breathtaking, shimmering beauty. Atop Kaye's whispering percussion, elegant fills from the string section, and Davis's masterful upright bass, which takes the lead, Morrison unleashes his finest vocal gymnastics, quivering and bellowing with emotion, and at times moving into sheer, wordless, blissful adoration. *Beside You*, with its twinkling dual guitars and diffuse structure, waxes between introspective melancholy and chest-beating anguish, while the stately, waltz-time *Sweet Thing* mixes naive yet evocative lines like "gardens all wet with rain" with passionate pillow talk. Morrison digs deep into his blues-shouter background for *Cyprus Avenue*, a rambling autobiographical piece, all seedy fiddle and trilling keyboards, as he howls at his searing memories.

Even the "poppiest" cut, *The Way Young Lovers Do*, boasts a hesitant, urban-waltz rhythm and a melody of remarkable complexity. Snatches of tight brass, the deranged jazz bass and the trombone solo lend this tale of a night of love a nervy Manhattan twist. *Madam George*, which follows, is the album's epic in every sense. Another saga from Cypress Avenue, it stretches across more than nine and a half minutes, through a series of carefully drawn observations of Madam George and the hopeless cases that surround her. When Morrison breaks into the repeated phrase "the love that loves to love", time seems to stands still. *Ballerina*, yet another song of love from one lonely soul to another, matches "Sweet Thing" for the beauty and purity of its desire. The cracked, deconstructed blues of the final cut, *Slim Slow Slider*, leans heavily on its clarinet accompaniment before the album finally collapses to a close.

In an echo of William Blake's *Songs Of Innocence And Experience*, the two sides of the original album were labelled "In The Beginning" and "Afterwards". For once, the parallel stands up; an enduring monument to Morrison's quality songcraft, *Astral Weeks* evinces all the love and despair of Blake at his most majestic.

⮞ We almost chose **A Night In San Francisco**, Polydor, 1994

# 54

# Neu!

## Neu!

Brain/United Artists, 1972

Klaus Dinger (vocals, drums, gtr), Michael Rother (gtr, bass, electronics).

When Klaus Dinger and Michael Rother formed Neu! in August 1971, they had already served their apprenticeship in Kraftwerk. Through live performances with that band, they'd laid the groundwork for what they went on to achieve – one of the absolute pinnacles of the phenomenal burst of musical creativity that took place in Germany in the late Sixties and early Seventies. The product of a four-day recording session in Conny Plank's legendary Cologne studio, the group's self-titled debut, **Neu!**, was as shockingly original as its red and white sleeve, which was starkly stamped with the band name in a direct pastiche of marketing-department sloganeering.

From the opening Hallogallo, it was apparent that something special had arrived; based on the stripped-down metronomic drumming of Dinger, and layered over with the circling, searingly minimal guitar lines of Rother, the almost entirely instrumental Neu! sound was precisely that – new – while simultaneously amounting to a re-examination of the very roots of the 4/4 heartbeat of rock'n'roll.

Dubbed "motorik" for its relentless road-movie drive – though Dinger preferred the terms "endlose" or "lange gerade" ("endless" and "long straight road" respectively), and now calls it "Apache" – the beat was an energetic trance rhythm of deceptive simplicity and stark beauty. However, the album had more variety to offer than raw beat; it also pioneered the abstracted, minimal bowed guitar and echoed cymbals of Sonderangebot, and the contemplative wah-pedal-melodies and circling drums of Weissensee, capable of building to restrained bursts of emotional release.

Side two was similarly inventive, opening with the "found sounds" of a rowing boat on Im Glück – recorded by Dinger on holiday with his Swedish muse Anita, to whom many of the songs were dedicated – which merged into another somnolent, gorgeous guitar line. That slowly rising and fading melody, abruptly interrupted by road-drills, is replaced by the loping bass and phased Japanese banjo (which becomes increasingly distressed and wayward) of Negativland, the definitive expression of the hypnotic, seemingly endless but ever-changing trademark Neu! groove. Here Plank's admirable sense of restraint shines through, reining in the duo's tendencies towards acoustic pyrotechnics and ensuring that the resulting dynamics are far more involving than the mere unhinged assault of noise. The closing Lieber Honig is one of the more strangely affecting love songs ever recorded, featuring the album's only (extremely hoarse) vocals from a Dinger who seems to be constantly on the verge of tears. Eventually, amid welling feedback, Rother's gently picked guitar trails away, and the sound of the boat on water returns, to provide a satisfyingly atmospheric conclusion.

Before re-emerging in the Nineties as lost classics in their own right, the three Neu! albums passed into underground legend, profoundly influencing artists like David Bowie – especially during his Berlin period, as heard on *Low* – and Sonic Youth (see "Two Cool Rock Chicks Listening To Neu!" on their 1988 *Ciccone Youth* album) along the way. Radio soundscape pranksters Negativland took their name from one track, Julian Cope remains a tireless fan, and Stereolab's early career bore the unmistakeable stamp of the motorik beat, which can also be discerned in the trance beats of early acid house. Neu! themselves remain one of the most neglected bands ever to contribute to the ongoing transformation of rock music.

➲ We almost chose **Neu! 1975**, Germanophon, 1975

# 55

# New York Dolls

## New York Dolls

Mercury, 1973

Sylvain Sylvain (gtr, pno, vocals), Johnny Thunders (gtr, vocals), David Johansen (harmonica, gong, vocals), Arthur Kane (bass), Jerry Nolan (drums).

With their first album, the New York Dolls encapsulated the notorious decadence of the Big Apple music scene at its early-Seventies peak. A year later, these faux-transvestite, druggy, made-up punks would be pin-up idols to thousands of screaming underage girl fans; soon after that, the whole thing blew up in their faces, in the form of rampant paranoia and death by substance abuse. Nonetheless, they were part of the advance guard who made possible not only punk, but also the reappraisal of good-times rock'n'roll, later in the decade. Recorded and mixed in less than a week, the **New York Dolls** album fizzles with hormones, bad behaviour, jealousy, and above all an overwhelming desire to be famous.

Before they even entered the studios, the Dolls lost one member, drummer Billy Murcia, to a drink- and drug-related mishap in London. Hightailing it home, they recruited Jerry Nolan, a vital improvement, as his replacement. Tensions were already rife. Frontman Sylvain Sylvain – himself no shrinking violet – had to contend with two other major egos, the scarcely-able-to-stand-up playing style of Johnny Thunders forever competing to draw attention away from the outrageous stagewear of David Johansen. Arthur "Killer" Kane was frequently too drunk to notice, while Nolan was happy simply to be playing and getting paid, so at least the rhythm section was solid, but producer Todd

Rundgren had his work cut out to pull the demoralized and bitching Dolls together, let alone create a masterpiece.

With the storming Personality Crisis, the album launches straight into a three-way duel between Thunders, Sylvain and Johansen, complete with frantic, John Cale-style piano, raw tough-drag singing, yob-hero guitar, and camp little touches like off-key backing vocals, and the nifty stop-start in the middle. This is grown-up glam, tinged with decay, and it continues through the sleaze of Looking For A Kiss and the urban warfare of Vietnamese Baby. A little light amid the gloom is cast by the breathy love song Lonely Planet Boy, with its lyrics of a teasing lover and Buddy Bowser's elegant sax, before the thunder'n'lightning of Frankenstein (orig) tramples the mood into the dirt with six minutes of power-riffing and reverb.

Trash, with its tag line of "How d'you call your lover boy?" is glam at its dirtiest and sweetest. An ode to cross-dressing, drug-taking and carrying a switchblade, it was a stomping rock'n'roll tribute to the pleasures of a bit of rough trade. Next comes Bad Girl (originally "Black Girl"), a tale of lust at first sight that's a bumping, grinding piece of pure New York sass, with Thunders grandstanding on guitar. For Subway Train he pulls out even more stops. With siren-effect guitars and a timeless opening riff that was to be a mainstay of Thunders' solo career, this celebration of drug-fuelled hedonism mutates, weirdly, into Someone's In The Kitchen With Dinah. Bo Diddley's Pills – all trashcan harp and dumb lyrics – includes the album's least convincing line, the tongue-in-cheek yell of "got me taking this junk against my will". On Private World, next, Johansen does his best Jagger impression through a tale of pressure and paranoia.

*New York Dolls* closes with Jet Boy, an everyday story of a New York where your partner may, at any moment, be stolen by a passing superhero. Held together by Nolan's drumming, this features the album's longest instrumental break. Clocking in at 45 seconds, it's an object lesson to the dinosaurs of progressive rock whom the Dolls helped to bring down.

⮑ We almost chose **Too Much Too Soon**, Mercury, 1974

# 56

# Nirvana

## Nevermind

Geffen, 1991

Kurt Cobain (vocals, gtr), David Grohl (drums, vocals), Chris Novoselic (bass, vocals), Kirk Canning (cello).

Despite being recorded when the band was on the brink of stardom, **Nevermind** reeks of impending disaster. In the interim, however, before Cobain lost control to heroin, and before the fame went sour, MTV took Smells Like Teen Spirit and exploded the band over a worldwide audience. *Nevermind* represents the high-water mark of grunge, combining state-of-the-art corporate rock production techniques with bleak Pacific Northwest nihilism and despair. Nirvana had a simple though devastatingly effective formula, in which restrained and self-revelatory verses were punctuated by wall-shaking, scream-laden choruses, and searing if technically simple guitar solos. The lyrics, a mumbled mess of sadness and depression, numbed by booze and industrial doses of illegal chemicals, gave a voice to anyone who needed to ask "what the hell am I trying to say?"

"Smells Like Teen Spirit" – the name taken from a deodorant aimed at the smelly adolescent market – was always going to be a hit. A brooding chord riff plays through once by itself, then the rest of the band revs up like a sports car and bursts into action. This song effectively wrote the book for grunge technicians, with full-on, in-the-teeth-of-a-gale vocals straining to make themselves heard over the poor suffering drums – themselves taking a hell of a pounding – and the dangerously overdriven guitars suddenly giving way to the peaceful yet terrifyingly exposed space at the eye of the storm, where a single-string two-note riff and drumbeat make room for Cobain's incoherent vocals. As well as giving up the album's title, the final line, "oh well, whatever, nevermind", encapsulates the slacker generation's philosophy. The same recipe works just as well in Drain You, itself peppered with numb, dumb "I don't care" lyrics.

Nirvana didn't just stare at their shoes and whine; they made great punk rock too. Songs like Breed – fast, simple and again boasting an "I don't care" motif – and Territorial Pissings – which, obscurely enough, copies the old, raw Slaughter And The Dogs sound – are prime slices of pulse-boosting, fist-in-the-air, raging rock'n'roll music. It has to be said, though, that the more thoughtful, gentler-paced numbers are in general the most powerful. In Bloom bubbles and fumes between bursts of angry noise, while the swirling mists of guitar on Come As You Are echo Blue Öyster Cult's "Don't Fear The Reaper".

Polly is Nevermind's bleakest and most harrowing track. Recorded elsewhere in their career as a faster, blink-and-you'll-miss it punk thrash, its shattered narrative of kidnapping, torture and rape is revealed here in small glimpses, which grow in brooding evil thanks to a slow, acoustic arrangement and the chilling lack of engagement of the narrator. The even slower Something In The Way has an equally unsettling mood, with lyrics such as "it's OK to fish 'cos they don't have any feelings" encapsulating the emotional blockage which Nirvana so eloquently described.

Cobain's little-boy-lost looks and soul-baring lyrics took the band straight to the hearts of a host of misunderstood teenagers. Nirvana's earlier work had been let down by sketchy production, while their later albums never captured this intoxicating mix of screaming defiance and tranquillized resignation. *Nevermind*, however, crystallized the mood of a moment, in a burst of bitter, righteous songwriting that was to have a profound impact on rock music for the rest of the century.

➲ We almost chose **In Utero**, Geffen, 1993

# 57

# Oasis

## Definitely Maybe

Creation, 1994

Liam Gallagher (vocals), Noel Gallagher (gtr, vocals), Paul Arthurs (gtr), Paul McGuigan (bass), Tony McCarroll (drums).

Each new generation has to rediscover the raw power of no-frills, electric-guitar-driven rock'n'roll for itself. In the Nineties, a pair of brothers from Manchester and their pals somehow managed to grab, with their thieving little hands, the pure elusive flame that had passed from Elvis to Lennon and Rotten. **Definitely Maybe**, the first Oasis album, is a classic of swaggering "who the hell are you?" self-confidence, mercifully free from the offensive arrogance that every star soon develops. In its celebration of the joys of living purely for the moment, it harks straight back to the mod operas of Pete Townshend and the intoxicated boogie of the Faces.

Having paid his dues roadying for Inspiral Carpets, Noel Gallagher elbowed his way into brother Liam's garage band by promising to make them rich and famous. Inspired by a heady blend of speed, hormones and adolescent stroppiness, the reconstituted band cobbled together a set of clean, cool songs. Shamelessly filching melodies, chord progressions, riffs, ideas, and influences from everyone from the Stones to the New Seekers, the end product was a collage, sure, but with forty years of good ideas to choose from, the band assembled a masterpiece, one of the most consistently exciting rock albums of the decade.

The opener, Rock'n'Roll Star, sets the tone. Both challenge and declaration of intent, it kicks off eleven tracks of breathtaking bad attitude, with all guns blazing and the amplification set to beyond the red line. A hymn to the sheer magic of being young, dumb and ready to burst with self-importance, it was instantly adopted nationwide as the essential mood-setting prelude to a Saturday night on the town. Shakermaker, which follows, takes its name from a depressing Seventies "'craft toy", its melody from a Coca-Cola commercial, and its guitar sounds from glitter pop bands. The yob psychedelia of the lyrics, and the trippy bottleneck guitar sound, marry Slade to Pink Floyd in a strangely compelling union.

Live Forever and Up In The Sky helped to establish the limited "sky", "fly", "shine", and "mine" vocabulary of Britpop. With essentially meaningless lyrics but rousing choruses and inspirational guitar solos, they add a modern hoodlum strut to the guitar lines of the Beatles, the Kinks and the Who. That spicy street-cred mix soon had the adolescent male market in the palms of Oasis' hands.

Columbia, Supersonic and Cigarettes & Alcohol are celebrations of "walking with the gods", which document the sheer fun of getting high with your friends, getting high with your lover, getting high to get over the disillusionment, and getting high just for the hell of it. Bring It On Down, on the other hand – a powerful slice of urban paranoia, bedecked with punk-rock drumming and guitars from the dark side of the Glitter Band – serves as a reminder of just how good Oasis can be as a straightforward rock'n'roll band. Digsy's Diner – the album's "Ringo track", a chirpy tale of ham-fisted attempts at seduction by means of cuisine – cleans the palate for the grand finale.

From the opening guitar riff, mangled irreparably in a million bedrooms, to the eminently yellable refrain, equally suited to lager frenzy or loved-up hugginess, the stoners' anthem, Slide Away, has "epic" written all over it. Technically, *Definitely Maybe* closes with the throwaway northern venom of Married with Children, as bitchy as Bowie in Berlin, but the curtain really falls as the final chords of "Slide Away" echo between your ears.

➲ We almost chose **(What's The Story) Morning Glory**, Creation, 1995

# 58

# The Orb

## The Orb's Adventures Beyond The Ultraworld

Big Life/Island, 1991

Alex Patterson (everything), Steve Hillage (gtr), Youth (bass), Thrash (engineer).

the orb's adventures beyond the ultraworld
double album

Unexpected consequences of the late-Eighties innovation in British clubland of setting aside chill-out rooms – refuges of relative peace, tucked away from the main dance floors – included the birth of ambient, a revived interest in dub reggae, and the emergence of acts like the Orb, whose work dispenses with recognizable instruments, structures and beats in the quest for a musical tranquillizer. Alex Patterson's eclectic musical knowledge – he worked as A&R man for EG Records, home to Eno and the mother lode of ambient – made him the perfect caretaker for the damaged souls who fell into his care at Paul Oakenfold's Land Of Oz club.

When he came to make his own music as the Orb, Patterson was able to call on a host of old pals, including thoroughbred hippy turned rave musician Steve Hillage; Killing Joke's former bassist turned producer, Youth; and KLF founder member Jimmy Cauty. Though labelled "ambient house", the music they created on **The Orb's Adventures Beyond The Ultraworld** has a long and distinguished history that dates back to the electronic landscapes of Tangerine Dream and, as is especially evident on Back Side Of The Moon, mid-Seventies Pink Floyd. Using humour, psychedelic mood-creating sounds, taped effects, loops and delays, the Orb's work echoes the Acid Tests of the late Sixties. Almost any of its tracks could accompany the galaxy-spanning final act of Kubrick's *2001*.

With the album extending over almost two hours, Patterson has ample time to construct a series of new worlds for fried brains to colonize, and to explore them in detail. Aided by Hillage's guest guitarwork and keyboard abuse, and Youth's trademark bassquake, he takes House music away from the body and into the mind, creating a dance music to lie down to. For the press presentation of *Adventures . . .*, London's music journalists were treated to sessions in flotation tanks; unsurprisingly, it was a critical hit. The formula – laid-back funk grooves, pretty samples from mother nature, and sound effects swimming in and out of the mix – was adopted elsewhere, and repeated by the Orb themselves, but never with the freshness seen here.

The first widely-known Orb release, A Huge Ever Growing Pulsating Brain That Rules From The Centre Of The Ultraworld, spread like a rash across the club scene, and landed the band their first John Peel radio session. It features here as a live mix, swelling with a sense of crystalline growth and packed with thought-provoking samples borrowed from a broad spectrum of disparate sources – most notably, the lift from Minnie Ripperton's "Loving You". The Pink Floyd connection swims to the surface once again when an incongruous clock-ticking rhythm breaks the floaty mood, cockerels crow, jets fly overhead, church bells ring, and an alarm clock shrills.

Little Fluffy Clouds demonstrates the awesome power of a couple of keyboards, a chest-collapsing bassline, and a sampler. Thanks to Jamie Lee Curtis' stoned-sounding vocals (plucked, out of context, from an interview) burbling about the beauties of nature, and samples lifted from Ennio Morricone's irresistible spaghetti-Western soundtracks, it's both danceable and smile-inducing.

The Orb make relaxing, positive, ready-to-use psychedelia for the Nineties. Coffee-table "druggy" music for a generation that has pretty much hung up its dancing trousers, it may be; but it's none the worse for that.

⮑ We almost chose **Blue Room**, Big Life, 1992

# 59

# Pavement

## Slanted And Enchanted

Big Cat, 1992

Stephen Malkmus (vocals, gtr), Scott Kannberg (gtr), Gary Young (drums).

Although their musical influences flew like a flag, the debut album from Pavement, **Slanted And Enchanted**, announced the band as a powerful voice in their own right. Set up by hometown boys Malkmus and Kannberg in Stockton, California, in 1989, Pavement were charter members of the lo-fi scene, as characterized by an empty, treble-heavy sound and oblique, image-rich lyrics. Their music was a tasty stew of the clever, introspective work of the Fall, Sonic Youth and the Pixies, plus a knowing, late-Eighties resignation and cynicism.

Building upon their underground reputation, *Slanted And Enchanted* turned heads, in the US and overseas, in a rock scene bloated by the nihilism of grunge. At first available only as a self-produced cassette, it was later released on vinyl and CD with a sleeve whose art-therapy collage and deranged handwritten look maintained the virulently indie-pendent feel, while doing little to suggest the magnificent merging of sunlit gentle music with hair-tearing, tortured-genius, guitar noise that lay within.

Pavement's music rarely touches on rock's usual "verse-chorus-verse" format; its structure depends instead on contrasting moods, and changes in pace, volume or rhythm. Thus the humour and panache of Summer Babe (Winter Version), in which the straightforward, chord-riff backing and deadpan vocals blithely ignore the guitar-hero soloing. There's a touching, if desperate, hopefulness to the solo, where the swaggering bravado somehow makes up for the lack of technical ability. This endearing mixture of wistful vocals, at times maddened with rage, and "so bad it's brilliant" guitar gave Pavement a vulnerability and intelligence often absent in an era of unthinking negativity.

Lyrically, Pavement tend towards the enigmatic, relying on fragmented imagery and violent emotional contrasts to generate moods that range from mellow contentment to eye-popping terror. Even the most extreme moments of *Slanted and Enchanted*, however, gain warmth and humanity from the quiet introspective interludes. Trigger Cut has an unvarying rhythm, with all instruments keeping to the same clockwork beat and a mood of controlled tension. The laconic, Velvet Underground drone of In The Mouth A Desert is lifted by hope, humour and hints of passion in the vocals, and machine-gun guitar chops.

Elsewhere, the band nod towards Captain Beefheart-style dysfunctional rock (as in Chesley's Little Wrists or Flame Throwa), or sleazy, end of the night, strip-club jazz (the vamping waltz-time Our Singer). There's stark poetry set to music in Perfume V ("shivered like a vein slashed bright and clean"), dirty shambling rock in Jackals, False Grails: The Lonesome Era, and demented Mark E. Smith boogie in Two States. No Life Singed Her blends Jesus And Mary Chain surf-punk guitar drone with bursts of frantic screaming, whereas Zurich Is Stained is a groovy, slide-guitar-led motor-cruise.

At its best, Pavement's music is so dense as to be almost impenetrable. Songs such as Loretta's Scars and Here suggest an overpowering impression that deadly personal secrets are being imparted, but remain perplexing even after repeated listening. Their intricately structured "manicured noise" approach, and their manifest sincerity, made Pavement one of the most important and influential bands of the Nineties. Picking up respect from their fellow musicians and from a growing audience, they continued with *Crooked Rain, Crooked Rain* (1994), *Wowee Zowee* (1995), and *Brighten the Corners* (1997), refining and cleaning up the sound but never outclassing this stunning opener.

➲ We almost chose **Crooked Rain, Crooked Rain**, Big Cat, 1994

# 60

## Pere Ubu

### The Modern Dance

Cooking Vinyl, 1978

David Thomas (vocals, pcn, musette), Tom Herman (gtr), Scott Krauss (drums), Tony Maimone (bass), Allen Ravenstine (synths, kbds).

Dark, powerful and quite unlike anything that had gone before, Pere Ubu's debut album, **The Modern Dance** is an at-times frightening blend of Beefheart-influenced jazzy rock and screaming urban punk. David Thomas' vision – the defining impulse behind the music – went on to influence the extreme sector of the rock world until the Nineties.

Originally put together by Thomas and guitarist Peter Laughner, both ex-members of Cleveland proto-punk band Rocket From The Tombs, Pere Ubu took their name, a deal of their surrealist imagery, and a heavy dose of wit from early twentieth-century Absurdist dramatist Alfred Jarry, author of the play *Ubu Roi*. While their instrumental assault tactics borrowed heavily from the Detroit crew – the MC5, Stooges et al – the ominous, disjointed sound they created was entirely their own. Although Laughner had left the band by the time the album was recorded, he was crucial to its development, and received writer's credit on Life Stinks. The track made a fitting epitaph when he died of a surfeit of excess a few years later.

Non Alignment Pact breaks *The Modern Dance* open with a fearsome warning-tone, before galloping off with a comparatively undemanding art-punk drum-plus-guitar thrash. Thomas' singing, however, is astonishing; he shrieks and warbles on the verge of hysteria over a backing that resembles the Stooges with a guest appearance from the deranged Roxy Music-era Brian Eno. Even now it remains distinctly unorthodox; on first hearing, back when standard 4/4 punk was still a novelty, it was breathtaking. It's followed by The Modern Dance itself, a disturbing collage of off-centre, "industrial" rhythms, and chanted vocals, using "found sound" fragments where a more traditional rock song would have instrumental breaks.

The Beefheart influence is at its most evident in Laughing, the third track, with its lengthy free-rock "noodling", rhythms broken at random, and lyrics peppered with dark humour. The loping, difficult-to-follow guitar riff and abstract vocals of Street Waves, next, show Pere Ubu as the missing link between the high-strangeness of San Francisco's Residents and the squalid artiness of Public Image Limited.

At the start of Chinese Radiation, a slow, vaguely "oriental"-sounding guitar line gives way to a strung-out, spacey synthesizer line, and, for once, gentle vocals from Thomas. Before long, however, the voice toughens up, the pace increases and soon Thomas is screaming for his life over frantic crowd noises.

"Life Stinks" crashes by in a blur of almost incoherent rage, its lyrics dripping despair – "I can't wait to die, I can't think because I need a drink. Life stinks", while every part of Real World oozes menace. Things hardly brighten up during Over My Head, where swooping keyboards back up a brooding acoustic guitar, and the only moment of light comes as cymbals briefly crash mid-song.

The sound of a slide projector shuffling through transparencies and violently shattering glassware provide the unorthodox percussion effects for Sentimental Journey before the downright odd squawks from the synth and doom-laden intoned vocals come into play. Add a sprinkle of Beefheart and the final, unsettling catalogue of possessions and voila!

The Modern Dance finishes with the vaguely tango-driven Humour Me, closing with the repeated mantra "That was fate, it's a joke" – an upsetting end to an always challenging album.

⊃ We almost chose **Dub Housing**, Rough Trade, 1978

# 61

# Pet Shop Boys

## Very

Parlophone, 1993

Neil Tennant (vocals, kbds), Chris Lowe (vocals, kbds).

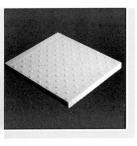

Neil Tennant once memorably dismissed the high-art pretensions of his contemporaries with the phrase "It's all just pop music". Nonetheless, with Chris Lowe, he has been creating thought-provoking, at times wistful, music for the best part of two decades. In addition to any number of irresistibly catchy, almost throwaway tunes, they've been responsible for art happenings, a series of stunning collaborations, and even an almost sacrilegious, campy, Vegas-style combination of U2's "Where The Streets Have No Name" with the Andy Williams classic "Can't Take My Eyes Off You". Masters of both irony and melody, the Pet Shop Boys combine synthesizer-based disco rhythms with bittersweet lyrics in a music of impeccable taste.

**Very**, their fifth studio album, was recorded after seven years at the top. Even though almost every sound is generated electronically, it sparkles with feeling and humanity. Certain cuts address hard-edged issues that range from homelessness to homosexual denial, but the majority deal with the most interesting aspects of love – how it all begins, how things start to go wrong, and how it ends. Having captured the breathless excitement and absurdity of a new romance in I Wouldn't Normally Do This Kind Of Thing, the Pet Shop Boys move on to reflect on the joys and the transience of love in both the calm of Liberation and the disco-heaven of One And One Make Five. A Different Point Of View re-works their trademark retro-disco sound for the Nineties, adding a healthy dose of techno-influenced "acid-squidge", while Tennant conjures up the most powerful vocal hook of the album. Despite the mood-elevating sounds, the lyric explores the recriminations and apologies that follow a lovers' argument. By One In A Million, the singer is searching desperately for a way to convince that special lover to stay. In the slower, more considered Dreaming Of The Queen, familiar "anxiety dream" images – nudity and ridicule in front of important people, in this case Queen Elizabeth and the already-iconic Princess Diana – convey the pain and desolation at love's end.

Serious themes are tackled from the first track, Can You Forgive Her, onwards. A moderately-paced melange of insomnia, tormented dreams and painful, shameful love, it deals with the notably non-pop subject of a man in a heterosexual relationship struggling to deny his own homosexuality. To Speak Is A Sin takes a cold look at the reptilian etiquette of cruising, while the controversial Young Offender recounts the lecherous yet tender stalking of an underaged lad through an urban amusement arcade. The narrative, which depicts being attracted by the dangers of "rough trade" like a moth to a neon sign, is punctuated by sound effects lifted from computer games. This willingness to look at the seedy side continues in Yesterday When I Was Mad, while The Theatre champions the young homeless who sleep in shop doorways in London's theatre district, with the help of a choir and the deranged sampled laughter of the Pet Shop Boys' other great city-life epic, 1984's "West End Girls".

Too much the showmen to leave their audience down and depressed, the Boys close *Very* with their version of Go West. Out-camping the original by miles – a considerable achievement considering the Village People's way with exaggerated stereotypes – this is the album's big production number, with sound effects of ocean waves and gulls, a hugely butch male voice choir, a brass section, and the wailing of a soul diva all laid on top.

⮑ We almost chose **Discography**, Parlophone, 1991

# 62

# Pink Floyd

## The Piper At The Gates Of Dawn

EMI, 1967

Syd Barrett (gtr, vocals), Roger Waters (bass, vocals), Rick Wright (organ, pno), Nicky Mason (drums).

The first British album to be produced by serious psychedelic explorers, **The Piper At The Gates Of Dawn** wrote the book for the rest of the "head" musicians in the UK. The Pink Floyd wove their way between childish whimsy and beautifully enunciated, university-educated lyrics, all topped with intricate structures and difficult melodies to distract the consciousness, to create a series of backgrounds, music for the inside of the eyeballs. Through techniques like varying the rhythm mid-song, or changing lyrical tack mid-verse, they conjured up both pastoral soundscapes and thrilling astral journeys.

The Floyd started out as a straightforward bluesy rock band; not the kind of act that generally confronted its audience with lyrics lifted directly from the I Ching, or tales of scarecrows come to life. Their secret ingredient came in the form of Barrett's already unusual view of the world, and his unique musical vision. *Piper* exhibits the prime characteristics of both the British and US schools of "acid rock", such as echoed vocals fading in and out over keyboard-laced backing, which itself ebbs and flows in intensity; esoteric lyrics of isolated, discrete phrases; and songs with lengthy, solo-filled, instrumental endings.

Most of its tracks aim, with varying success, to mimic some aspect of the LSD trip. Let There Be More Light, for example, displays the everyday world – as represented by sound effects of office machinery and a droning guitar riff – dwindling in relevance as the trip comes on, while the riff slowly disappears behind noodling organ patterns. Just as acid comes in waves of intensity, patterns start to emerge from the instrumental wash. Spacey, magical lyrics come and go between whispered hints to "be aware", before control is finally relinquished to a long instrumental. In Pow R Toc H, voices are used to create percussive effects and to chant over a piano and acoustic guitar jam. Individual musical strands grow and diminish in the mix, leading the mind towards inner space. Stethoscope and Bike capture the best of the acid experience – heart-pounding excitement, humour and adolescent giggling, which swerve sideways into moments of wide-eyed worship tinged with lust.

The lack of lyrics on the standout track, Interstellar Overdrive, is more than compensated for by its space-opera title. It gains further psychedelic weight as first the guitars and then the keyboards peel off to explore, held together only by the desperate concentration of the rhythm section. Soon even the drum and bass axis gives way, to leave us confronted by the vastness of the universe. For an instant we glimpse the void, as silence, broken only by sonar-like beeps, takes over. Rolling drums slowly bring us down, collecting our thoughts en route back to the final "thank you and goodnight" triumphal ending.

Barrett, an early "acid casualty", was manoeuvred out of the Floyd shortly after *Piper*'s release. His solo career smothered by his mental problems, he retired into the backstreets of Cambridge, having taken the band to the brink of international success. Their second album, *A Saucerful Of Secrets*, was riddled with his influence, and consolidated their position as Europe's prime psychonauts. Without his gentle hand at the controls, the band turned to film scores and concept albums, then mutated into the ultimate coffee-table tripsters with their world-dominating exploration of mental illness, *Dark Side Of The Moon*, in 1973. Thirty years on, they remain the world's top acid-rock band, but they've yet to better their debut outing.

➲ We almost chose **A Saucerful of Secrets**, EMI, 1968

# 63

## Pixies

# Trompe Le Monde

4AD, 1991

Black Francis (gtr, vocals), Kim Deal (bass, vocals), Eric Drew Feldman (kbds), Jeff Feldman (dumbek, pcn, tabla), David Lovering (drums), Joey Santiago (gtr).

**Trompe Le Monde** provides a faithful record of the moment when the Pixies' blend of plastic and shimmer with distortion and rant reached its peak. Yes, 1988's *Surfer Rosa* and 1989's *Doolittle* were both in their ways more influential on the explosion of "alternative" bands who followed in the Pixies' wake, while *Trompe Le Monde* goes out of its way to mock the imitators, but for that very reason it's a harder-edged, more fully realized artefact.

Where Steve Albini's production on *Surfer Rosa* had been largely responsible for turning the Pixies into indie gods, Gil Norton set out on *Trompe Le Monde* to re-cast them as stadium rock stars. Had the album come out a year later, with a few more terrace chants, some obvious stop-start dynamics, and a fatter, wider, synth-woosh sound, it might have made Norton the Mutt Lange of the Nineties. As it is, despite its punishing riffs and abundant hooks, *Trompe Le Monde* never took off, and the band broke up shortly after its release. Singer-guitarist Black Francis re-named himself Frank Black, and with *Frank Black* and *Teenager Of The Year* began to release solo albums in substantially the same vein.

*Trompe Le Monde* displayed all the crankiness, rugged invidualism, and transparent disgust with the subculture, sex, white liberals, and life in general that were to characterize Black's records.

On top of that, it lacked the siren counterpoint which Kim Deal had supplied to Francis' epic whine on earlier Pixies material like "Gigantic" and "Here Comes My Man". Unlike the Frank Black records, though, *Trompe Le Monde* boasted tunes galore, felt like it still believed in rock'n'roll, and didn't sound like it was being sung by the Michael Douglas character in *Falling Down*.

While as ever couched in obtuse, often cryptic language, Black Francis' obsessions with aliens and trash were presented with sufficient melodic appeal and punk immediacy to bring them out of the cranks' ghetto. Alec Eiffel was, and still is, the best song ever written about architecture and thinking big, while Bird Dream of the Olympus Mons and The Navajo Know blended annihilation and space exploration, with echoes of *Doolittle*'s "Monkey Gone to Heaven". Even hate-fests like Subbacultcha and U-Mass channelled enough of their spleen through the guitar white-outs to make them work as air-punchers at your local ten-thousand-seat arena.

Unlike most indie rockers, the Pixies could riff as well as they could flip out. Planet of Sound, The Sad Punk and Head On wedded punk's catharsis of fury to rock's galvanizing peacock strut. All that "U-Mass" needed was a cowbell to go along with the Charlie Watts beat and buried harmonica, while "Subbacultcha" was a re-write of Jonathan Richman's "Pablo Picasso", with a little extra Link Wray kick, and the loathing projected on an entire culture instead of a rejecting girl. In addition, there was a mean Nico impression on "The Sad Punk", Distance Equals Rate Times Time droned more effectively than any band since the Velvet Underground, and Lovely Day possessed an amiable bounce, albeit undercut by slightly sinister lyrics, that was reminiscent of some of those Sixties garage bands featured on the *Nuggets* albums.

Motorway to Roswell was pretty silly, and didn't mean to be, but its off-kilter lustre perfectly embodied the Pixies' marriage of style, substance and obscurism. Unfortunately, it also showed where Francis' head was at.

➲ We almost chose **Doolittle**, 4AD/Elektra, 1989

# 64

# PJ Harvey

## Dry

Too Pure, 1992

Polly Jean Harvey (vocals, gtr, violin), Steve Vaughan (bass), Robert Ellis (drums, vocals, harmonium).

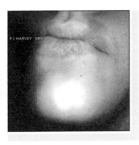

With songs that simmer and brood before they finally explode – much like the resentments and arguments that break up relationships – **Dry** offers a unique take on the thunder and lightning of grunge. Distinctly British and with a female perspective derived from Polly Harvey's lyrical and vocal input, it's an exploration of the extremes of lust, love, anger, and hatred that leaves little room for quiet affection or gentle reproach. The album confronts the demands of male-female relationships with the same steely intensity with which it celebrates the rewards they offer.

The dominant theme of raw, unfettered womanhood sits uncomfortably with *Dry*'s other main preoccupation, the perceived need for male approbation. The resultant friction contributes to a sensation of barely controlled frustration, which periodically boils over into raging gales of guitar-driven release.

From the opening track, Oh My Lover, with its stumbling rhythm and wary vocals, through O Stella, all white-funky, Red Hot Chili Peppers-style riffing, and on to its dying moments, *Dry* pushes images of love that burns, misery that cuts deep, contrition, seduction and pride.

Dress, which had been released as a single before the album appeared, reeks of fear. It depicts a cowed and confused Harvey searching desperately for approval ("must be some way I can dress to please him"). With the sound boosted by the addition of a bass guitar (Ian Olliver) and a double bass (Ben Groenenvelt), she finds it hard to walk in the clothes she wears. In a metaphor for love that's been trampled, the clothes become soiled and torn. Victory, which follows is, by contrast, a dimly lit and swampy groove.

The disturbing Happy And Bleeding follows, once again blending images of love and subjugation. It sits awkwardly alongside Sheela Na Gig, another pre-album single which celebrates righteously enraged womanhood and is vividly illuminated by contrasting moments of noise and calm. Taking its name from the ancient Celtic image of a naked woman with her knees held wide apart, and its two-chord powerhouse riff from the Velvet Underground school, it defiantly echoes "I'm gonna wash that man right out of my hair" from the musical *South Pacific*.

Hair reprises scenes from the Biblical story of Samson and Delilah over a complex guitar and drum pattern, then leads into the rich imagery of Joe, which is almost washed away by the demented thrash metal riff and Harvey's wailing delivery. On Plants And Rags, however, with additional guitar by Mike Paine, the eerie lyrics cut right through the mix. Charles Dickie's cello part is almost frightening.

Fountain is another desperate tale of sex and loss, told over a brooding, restrained guitar line. It leads into the big finale, Water, which boasts an intricate, staggering guitar riff, unfathomable lyrics that hint at divinity and suicide, and a slow swelling from its almost whispered introduction to a final cataclysm that leaves the ears ringing and pulse racing.

For the most part, *Dry* has a close, confessional feeling and an air of sanity on the verge of collapse. Stripped down to bare bones, the music maintains a respectful distance, giving the thoughtful images and cries of outrage in the songs the opportunity to penetrate and remain in the mind. When Harvey and the band let rip, they created a sound of elemental power.

➲ We almost chose **To Bring You My Love**, Island, 1995

# 65

# Iggy Pop

## Lust For Life

RCA, 1977

Iggy Pop (vocals), Carlos Alomar (gtr, vocals), Ricky Gardiner (gtr, vocals), Hunt Sales (drums, vocals), Tony Sales (bass, vocals), David Bowie (pno, vocals).

The Outsider is a rock'n'roll archetype. During the Seventies, characters such as Patti Smith, Johnny Thunders and Iggy Pop took it upon themselves to explore the limits of society, and then venture beyond. Together they documented and celebrated broken taboos, tried the unusual and the dangerous, and came back to tell the tale. By encouraging others to explore, by offering warnings and the potential for redemption, Iggy, the prime outsider, put himself through Hell and Heaven in 1977, the year in which he created both *The Idiot* – a darkside, stumblebum document of excess – and **Lust For Life** – a clear-eyed, focused beam of cocaine sunshine and vodka-fuelled joy.

For Iggy, redemption was never going to mean cleaning up completely. However, while he was still deriving a great deal of his energy, enthusiasm and inspiration from Latin America's prime export, there was no doubt that he'd been saved by Bowie and Berlin.

Opening with Lust for Life itself (a name shared with the movie biography of fellow troubled artist Vincent Van Gogh), Iggy nails his colours to his forehead as he jeers and swaggers through a declaration of good intent. The band stomps along behind the new improved Iggy, who's "done sleeping on the sidewalk", but who's still using chemicals and who's still a danger to right-thinking folk everywhere. The track pounds with joy, while Iggy rides the edge of madness, screaming with laughter that he's "worth a million in prizes".

Having turned his back on the cocktail of downers that had been his choice for the previous few years, Iggy was certainly feeling the sap rise. In Sixteen, Some Weird Sin (the outsider anthem) and Fall In Love With Me, he bellows animal desire, out-Jaggering Mick in sheer torment and celebrating the comforts of the odd pharmaceutical relapse. Sashaying along like strip-club routines, with honky-tonk piano touches and echoes of the Stooges' "I Wanna Be Your Dog" – plus vague hints of barely repressed urges to get a baby prostitute drunk before a session of unspeakable desires – these songs, together with The Passenger and Neighbourhood Threat are snapshots from Berlin's decadent Thirties' past, dragged into a Seventies rockstar debauch. Consciously acting out William S Burroughs' passionless descriptions of the junkie life, Iggy and David insulated themselves with powder and limousines from urban street life, riding through the city's ripped back side as isolated observers.

With its good-times call-and-response vocals, Success, however, echoes the opening track for sheer eye-twinkling mischief. Its swaggering guitar riffs, clapping and general merriment are inspirational. Turn Blue, by contrast, is harrowing. The most powerful, albeit instrumentally understated, track on the album displays Iggy at his most confessional, his "just say no" moment. Taking both title and subject matter from the language of heroin overdose, this is part narrative, part potential death-bed memoir, bursting with the soft explosive epiphany of a hit. The phrase "Jesus, this is Iggy" takes us past the "I can see God" stage, beyond even the "talking to God" stage, to reveal the choked-to-death-on-my-own-vomit stage that's just around the corner. Despite his least convincing line ("Mama, I didn't know what I was doing"), Iggy makes us watch while he shoots himself up. Holding our breath with him as he lets go the tie, we see that, as the track comes to a dead stop, he's also shot himself down.

➲ We almost chose **TV Eye**, RCA, 1978

# 66

# Elvis Presley

## Sunrise

RCA, 1999

Elvis Presley (gtr, vocals), Scotty Moore (gtr), Bill Black (bass).

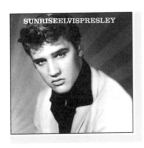

Make no mistake, this is the disc that started it all. It's impossible to imagine the modern world without Elvis, and it was the songs collected on the appropriately named **Sunrise** that launched his career and created the myth. When Elvis, Scotty Moore and Bill Black started fooling around with Arthur "Big Boy" Crudup's That's Alright Mama in a break during their first recording session for Sun Records on July 5, 1954, they can have had little inkling that they were inventing rock'n'roll as we know it. Sun Records owner Sam Phillips, however, knew immediately that he was onto something big. A longtime champion of black r'n'b, he realised that here was a completely new interpretation of an old blues classic – an interpretation that drew as much from white country and western traditions as it did from the blues, and had the potential to cross America's race divide and appeal to a white audience. The impact of such a fusion of black and white was earthshaking. As Scotty said of the music that Phillips recorded that day, "It was just so completely different . . . We just sort of shook our heads and said, well that's fine, but good God, they'll run us out of town!"

Over the next few days, Elvis and his band hit upon a startling transformation of Bill Monroe's bluegrass waltz, Blue Moon of Kentucky, which evolved from a slow, bluesy lament to a high-spirited declaration of self-discovery. In the recordings that followed, the nineteen-year-old Elvis drew upon all the sounds that he had ever heard – blues, gospel, hillbilly, pop, crooning, doo wop – and distilled them into something new and revolutionary. The arrangements were fresh and bursting with energy, while Elvis' voice soared, a unique mixture of innocence and sexual yearning.

"That's Alright, Mama", with its flipside Blue Moon of Kentucky, was Elvis' first single, and was a runaway success. There had been rock'n'roll hits before – "Rock Around The Clock" was already in the charts – but no one crystallized teenage sexuality like Elvis. As he toured the Deep South, playing almost 200 dates in twelve months, Elvis caused near-riots wherever he went. If his green coat, pink shirt and playful sneer didn't drive the girls wild, his pelvic gyrations caused mass hysteria. Scotty and Bill tried to keep up above the screams – as Scotty said, "we were the only band in history that was directed by an ass".

When Elvis first came to Sun, he was an inspired amateur. By the time he left for RCA, in November 1955, he was a phenomenon. Incendiary singles of Baby, Let's Play House, Mystery Train and Blue Moon had cemented his reputation. I Forgot To Remember To Forget became his first number one in the national country and western charts, and allowed his new manager "Colonel" Tom Parker to negotiate what was then the biggest advance ever known, $35,000, from RCA.

The Sun sessions laid the groundwork for his future success, but Elvis arguably never again achieved the spontaneity and sense of exhilaration that marked those early recordings. Of course, they were not released as an album as such at the time; it wasn't until 1987 that the Sun sessions were available on one disc. 1999's double CD *Sunrise* contains all this and more – a bonus disc containing some punchy alternate takes, half a dozen appallingly recorded live outtakes, and even My Happiness, the demo he made for his mother in 1953. It all has a raw, timeless beauty unequalled in popular music. Indispensable.

⮑ We almost chose **The Great Performances**, RCA, 1990

# 67

# The Pretenders

## Pretenders

Sire, 1980

Chrissie Hynde (gtr, vocals), James Honeyman Scott (gtr), Pete Farndon (bass), Martin Chambers (drums).

More than any other woman in rock, Chrissie Hynde understood that rock was all about attitude. Avoiding the usual poses adopted by distaff rockers – ice queen (Nico and Debbie Harry), arty singer-songwriter (Joni Mitchell, Kate Bush), psychedelic earth mother (Janis Joplin, Grace Slick), jail bait (the Runaways), gum-snapping tough chick (Joan Jett, Pat Benatar), artful psychotic (PJ Harvey, Kim Gordon), avant-gardist (Patti Smith, Yoko Ono) – Hynde grabbed the genre conventions of rock by the short and curlies, and turned them upside down. Joining the role-playing game of cock-rock on her own terms, Hynde subverted it without sacrificing its vital force.

After growing up in a dying industrial town in the rust belt of the American Midwest, Chrissie Hynde escaped a life of listening to Bachman Turner Overdrive by moving to England in the early Seventies. She soon started writing for the *NME*, and joined various bands at the dawn of punk, forming the Pretenders with Farndon, Chambers and Honeyman Scott in 1978. Their first single, 1979's **Stop Your Sobbing**, was produced by Nick Lowe. Its jingle-jangle guitars and quasi-Motown aesthetic helped to define the sound of the new wave, and a debut album, **Pretenders**, followed the next year.

While the Pretenders were clearly Hynde's band, their early success owed much to Honeyman Scott's guitar work, which fused the aggression of punk with the high production values, and feel for a riff, of the best chart pop. *Pretenders* was one of the few albums to bridge the new wave and the mainstream, and its slightly sterile reggae licks and highly processed guitar distortion became production hallmarks of early Eighties rock.

The highlight, Tattooed Love Boys, boasted a rhythm that was surely the blueprint for the Burundi-beat antics of Bow Wow Wow and Adam and the Ants. A tale of a girl exploring sex for the first time and discovering its potential brutality, it was the ultimate expression of Hynde's tip-toeing along the thin line between love and hate. After the guitar interlude, which mocked every cock-rock riff you can think of before sputtering out in the funniest evocation of the male orgasm ever, Hynde's new-found prowess means that she had gained the upper hand on her erstwhile sexual conquistador and "had [him] where [she] used to lay". A before-the-fact combination of the violent sexuality of both the Rolling Stones and Bikini Kill, "Tattooed Love Boys" was like a Rainer Werner Fassbinder film with the hooks and budget for pyrotechnics of a Hollywood action flick.

The other out-and-out rockers were almost as good. Precious was another ass-kicking sexual-adventure-cum-assertiveness-parable with one of the great "fuck off"s in music history, while The Wait was a perfect agglomeration of a choked guitar lick, an epic Pete Townshend-style windmill riff, and catalytic bass runs. Mystery Achievement, meanwhile, created what would soon become the band's trademark. The bass and drum interplay underneath a simple riff became the Pretenders' staple arrangement on later albums and Hynde's survivor's story would be the stuff of the band's other masterpiece, 1983's *Learning to Crawl*.

It was the ballads, however, that originally got the Pretenders noticed. All their first three singles – "Stop Your Sobbing", Kid and Brass in Pocket, all on *Pretenders* – were slow numbers that received fulsome praise in the music press. "Brass in Pocket", the most noteworthy, embodies the twin poles that drove Hynde's best songs: a surrender to desire and a proud independence.

⮕ We almost chose **The Singles**, Real, 1987

# 68

# Primal Scream

## Screamadelica

1991, Creation

Bobby Gillespie (vocals), Andrew Innes (gtr), Robert Young (gtr), Jah Wobble (vocals), Denise Johnson (vocals), The Orb (producer), Hypnotone (producer), Jimmy Miller (producer), Hugo Nicholson (producer), Andrew Weatherall (producer).

The early Nineties witnessed a renaissance in British rock, as indie bands used ecstasy to get in touch with their funky inner selves. While one pill too many prompted a few past-their-prime rock'n'roll embarrassments, the period also spawned some genuinely inspired artefacts. Primal Scream's **Screamadelica**, the most popular and influential dance/rock album of the decade, introduced a new hybrid sound that carried rock far off the old beaten track. Much of the credit belongs to acid-house prime mover Andrew Weatherall and his fellow producers, who provided dance-culture credibility as well as specific instrumental innovations like the use of brass and house-style piano. Major input from Gillespie et al included their notorious taste for chemicals and the wild side of life.

*Screamadelica*'s opener, Moving On Up, is a Keef-style funk-up. Its air of decadent excess owes much to Jimmy Miller, who worked with the Stones on *Sticky Fingers*, and also took the controls for Damaged, which oozes smack and regret. Slip Inside This House was a hit for the 13th Floor Elevators. Here, given a sitar backing and a white funk groove, it becomes a wide-eyed stoned meditation. Next up, the spectacular Don't Fight It, Feel It throbs with deep, tremor-inducing bass, and thrills with Denise Johnson's diva-like wailing.

Higher Than The Sun appears twice. The first version,

mixed by the Orb, is punctuated by quiet explosions and lost in reverb. On this mix the lyrics are readily decipherable, full of phrases like "drift in inner space" to aid the psychedelic pilgrim along the path. Later on comes the vastly trippier "dub symphony in two parts", jointly produced by the Weatherall/Nicholson Boy's Own Productions team and Jah Wobble. Here the only recognizable phrase is the title, while the rest of the vocal track is looped and dubbed beyond recognition, re-assembled into meaningless isolated syllables. By the time Wobble takes over for the second part, no trace of the original voice remains.

Inner Flight follows the Orb production of "Higher . . . " as a final phase of the trip, with its delicately twinkling keyboards and vocals floating far above the percussion. Then Come Together pulls us out of our reverie into a demonstration of unity. Rich in vocal samples, the song grows into a dance-protest for the rave generation. The production calls in church-style organ, evangelical hand-clapping, police sirens and the ominous soundbite "Brothers and Sisters, the name of the game is power!", to create a streetwise call to fight for the right to party.

The sublime Loaded, with its sample from *The Wild Bunch*, declares "We're gonna get loaded, we're gonna have a good time"; as fresh as ever, it remains a guaranteed dance floor filler. I'm Coming Down goes no distance at all to disguise its drug-related subject matter. With its languid sax line and "drifting, drifting" lyric, it's surprisingly reminiscent of the "I've been stoned before" motif of Anglo-French hippys Gong. A snapshot of fleeting determination to stop the chemical abuse – "powders and pills won't cure my ills, but they make me feel better for a while" – it's a stark, poetic summation of the hedonist manifesto.

Shine Like Stars, however, the track that closes *Screamadelica*, sees a return to wonderland. Its sense of stoned bewilderment and adoration – "I watch you dance, you look so happy" – perfectly captures the eye-opening worship, stronger even than everyday love, that can be found in a piece of blotting paper.

⮑ We almost chose **Give Out But Don't Give Up**, Creation, 1994

# 69

# Prince

## Sign O The Times

Paisley Park Records, 1987

Prince (everything), Wendy Melvoin (gtr, vocals), Lisa Coleman (flute, sitar, vocals).

The Artist Formerly Known As Prince – and also formerly widely hailed as a genius – was the leading musical figure of the Eighties. How the mighty are fallen. He now cuts a sad figure, making triple albums that nobody wants to hear (let alone buy), without even a name to his, er, name. Nevertheless, at his peak, Prince articulated a vision that re-interpreted his influences – soul, gospel, pop, house, to name but a few – for the digital age. Above all, he made funk mainstream, and hip beyond the dreams of Sly Stone and George Clinton.

Released in March 1987, **Sign O The Times** was not Prince's most adventurous album, but it was by far his most consistent. Originally conceived as a double album called *Dream Factory*, with the Revolution, the project metamorphosed into a triple set entitled *Crystal Ball*, and then, when Warner took fright, reverted back into a double disc, composed, arranged, produced, and largely performed by Prince alone. Half of *Sign O The Times* in its final form was recorded in his Minneapolis basement, with occasional contributions from Sheila E plus Wendy and Lisa; the rest was laid down in LA. All in all, it's a tour de force of musicianship, and it remains one of the very few double albums by any artist that holds up over four sides.

Although most of the tracks on *Sign O The Times* revolve, predictably, around Prince's sexual obsessions, the songs with other concerns have the most impact. The Curtis-Mayfield-styled opening track, Sign O The Times, is his strongest social statement. "He had begun to see the effects of crack and drugs on young people", said Alan Leeds of Prince's Paisley Park Records. "He's not really a preacher, but it's certainly an anti-drug song." The Cross, on the other hand, is a religious anthem. "Don't cry, He is coming / Don't die without knowing the Cross" he wails with feverish sincerity over layers of Hendrix-style guitar.

To guarantee a rich range of rhythms and emotions, Prince had no scruples about dipping into many diverse styles. Standout tracks include the fanciful Starfish and Coffee, breezy light pop that's as wacky as it is irresistible; the smouldering ballad Slow Love, reeking of Smokey and Marvin at their most seductive; and I Could Never Take The Place Of Your Man, with its extraordinary psychedelic middle section. There's exhilarating dance music too: the steamy funk of Hot Thing, the relentless Housequake, the nine-minute live take of It's Gonna Be A Beautiful Night, recorded in front of six thousand ecstatic Parisians. U Got The Look, one of several hits, featured an unlikely duet with Scottish songstress Sheena Easton (for whom Prince had already written the banned hit "Sugar Walls").

Sign O The Times even spawned a decent movie – live footage of the accompanying tour – that went some way to restoring Prince's celluloid reputation after the disaster of 1986's Under The Cherry Moon. The soundtrack album had had its moments of brilliance ('Kiss', the menacing "Anotherloverholenyohead", the sublime "Sometimes It Snows In April") but too much of it sounded like incidental movie music (which, of course, it was).

Sign O The Times proved that Prince was still on track – at least for the moment. However, his next official album, 1988's Lovesexy, was neither particularly inventive or commercial, and sold badly. Most of the Nineties have been spent on autopilot, although his ability to pull off the occasional brilliant single, such as 1994's "The Most Beautiful Girl In The World", suggests that it would be unwise to write him off.

➲ We almost chose **Purple Rain**, Warner, 1984

# 70

# The Prodigy

## Fat Of The Land

XL, 1997

Liam Howlett (mixing), Keith Flint (vocals), Maxim (vocals), Kool Keith (vocals), Saffron (vocals), Crispian Mills (vocals), Shahin Bada (vocals), Jim Davies (gtr).

The Prodigy has been more successful than any other act of the Nineties in marrying traditional rock to dance-orientated sounds, and never more so than on the groundbreaking **Fat of the Land**. Formed in 1991 in the ominously named Essex town of Braintree, they were originally an unassuming band who first became known for impish, instantly accessible, hardcore tunes like "Charly", which included a sample from a government child-safety film and took them to number three in the UK pop charts. That track spawned a host of imitations, featuring samples taken, with varying degrees of wit, from children's TV and other kiddy favourites.

Liam Howlett, the Prodigy's creative mainstay, was not so much a pill-popping weekender as a wannabe B-boy, with a taste for obscure hip-hop and the music made by the wild men of Jamaican reggae. He worked out the essential requirements for a killer dance track, and spent the next six years crafting his own distinctive, hard-edged sound. Sub-sub-bass detonations and floor-shaking keyboard effects were blended with pounding drums and raw, bleeding, rock guitar noise; great for dancing, equally brilliant for heads-down hairshaking rituals.

Meanwhile, the band were developing as live performers. Keith Flint transformed himself from floppy-hatted rave dancer to pierced, charismatic, green-haired frontman; Leroy Thornhill prowled the stage, bare chested and frankly disturbing in cat-eye contact lenses; and Maxim Reality was a large, looming presence to one side. During the run-up to *Fat Of The Land*, The Prodigy could do little wrong.

For all its irresistible energy, however, the first single from the album, Smack My Bitch Up, landed the band in serious controversy. Adopting as its refrain a couple of lines from underground heroes the Ultramagnetic MCs – also used by De La Soul on their *Buhloone Mindstate* album – the song was widely assumed to condone violence against women, and launched an anti-Prodigy backlash. Howlett responded that it was just a cool-sounding sample, which fit the beats he was working on in much the same way as his cheeky lift from the Art Of Noise.

Musically speaking, Breathe was cast on similar lines, maintaining its lengthy, tension-building intro with beats, guitars, sub-bass frequencies and other effects (this time, clashing swords and breaking glass). Diesel Power, more of an old-school rap track, lumbered forward like some gigantic earth-moving machine, before the manic laughter and shoutalong intensity of Funky Shit and the cartoon-horror of Serial Thrilla. Firestarter, another crowd-pleasing, stomp-generating, scream-fest of a single - with another lift from the Art Of Noise - added the image of Keith Flint's metal-filled, multi-hued head to the nightmare vocabulary of MTV viewers worldwide.

The less frenetic, mildly paranoid Mindfields draws comparisons between venturing behind enemy lines and the chemically fuelled internal explorations of the audience. With its unsettling mid-way change of pace, it unexpectedly reveals a more thoughtful Prodge, dealing with darker themes than usual. Narayan too, with guest vocals from Crispian Mills (of mystic popsters Kula Shaker), speaks of a long and perilous psychic voyage, helped by the extended drum solo that ends the track.

*Fat Of The Land* melded rock'n'roll bad attitude with the devil's own un-sit-downable dance beats, to create a consummate fusion of new technology and old-school swagger.

➲ We almost chose **Music for the Jilted Generation**, XL, 1994

# 71

# Public Image Ltd

## Metal Box / Second Edition

Virgin, 1979

John Lydon (vocals), Keith Levene (gtr, vocals), Jah Wobble (bass).

John Lydon was the only survivor of the Sex Pistols to emerge with any dignity. While his former cohorts descended into self-parody or worse, Lydon hooked up with a bunch of friends back in London. Towards the end of 1978, they released "Public Image", one of the great late-punk cries of anger. The album that followed (very punk, full of bitterness, and still available as *Compact Disc*) allowed Lydon time and space to rid himself of his demons. Although cathartic for all concerned, it was not much of a step forward.

The jagged rhythms of **Metal Box / Second Edition**, however, opened a whole new chapter of "art punk", inspiring bands like the Pop Group and This Heat to deconstruct sensuous dance music and reassemble a stark, soulless, industrial funk from its components. It was initially issued as a highly impractical but eminently collectible set of three twelve-inch singles, supplied in what appeared to be a cine-film canister with no pictures of the band and only a flimsy slip of paper to give bare details of personnel and track listing; Public Image Limited were playing the role of the anti-pop group. The *Metal Box* packaging was always a short-term limited edition, however, and the album was re-published as *Second Edition* in a conventional format soon after.

PIL's music derives much of its urgency from the neurotic disco beat and edgy tremolo guitar. The ten-and-a-half-minute tormented disco groove of Albatross introduces Lydon's new voice – an other-worldly, sub-Arabic wailing – while Levene investigates percussion guitar, Wobble's bass keeps the relentless jerking in step, and eerie studio effects combine to create something quite frightening. Like the epics of Lydon's heroes, Can, or the Velvet Underground, it never seems over-long. There's always enough happening, either instrumentally or in the lyrics, to grab the attention.

Swan Lake, previously issued as the "Death Disco" single, pulls its melody straight from Tchaikovsky, then hammers it down to a disco beat. Lydon screams full volume over straining guitar lines and explosions of bass, but the cheesy, synthesized strings ultimately drown out all the other disjointed sounds in a flood of peace. The disturbing Poptones, next, is characterized by a circling guitar riff and the unsettling treatment afforded Lydon's already-weird vocalizing of its typically oblique lyrics.

No Birds features a Can-influenced beat that fights against Lydon's melody-avoiding stretched-out vocal tactics. Harking back to Gong's Shakti Yoni and her "space-whisper", this piece employs the Lydon voice as much as an extra instrument as it does to impart words. Wobble takes centre-stage with wall-shaking bass and menacing narcotic singing for The Suit, while Bad Baby echoes "Fodderstompf" from the first PIL album with its cheeky "stop, stop, start again" false introduction. The album's final tracks, Socialist, Chant and Radio 4 segue one into the other in what is effectively a single instrumental. The "Radio 4" section – echoed years later in the Happy Mondays' "Harmony" – uses synthesized strings and a pretty bass melody to bring the entire twisted set to a gentle conclusion.

Public Image Limited remained at the cutting edge of post-punk during the Eighties, even charting in 1983 with "This Is Not A Love Song", baiting the media and challenging the audience to think for itself. Lydon only officially retired the band in 1993, but after Levene's departure in 1982, it was increasingly Johnny's show; impressive, but never as magical and free.

⮑ We almost chose **Plastic Box**, Virgin, 1999

# 72

# Pulp

## Different Class

Island, 1995

Jarvis Cocker (vocal, synth, gtr, mellotron), Nick Banks (pcn, drums), Candida Doyle (kbds), Steve Mackey (bass), Russell Senior (gtr, violin), Matthew Vaughan (programming), Mark Haley (programming), Mark Webber (guitar, kbds).

It may have taken fourteen years for Pulp to crack it, but in the end success came suddenly. With the release of **Different Class**, in 1995, they found themselves swept up in the fervour of Britpop and dumped unceremoniously centre-stage. Instant stardom, focused especially on frontman Jarvis Cocker, arrived on the back of two singles extracted from Pulp's previous album, *His'n'Hers*: the frenetic "Babies", and the voyeuristic "Do You Remember The First Time", which described hiding in a sister's wardrobe, observing her antics with her boyfriends. Not exactly good clean fun, perhaps, but Cocker's challenging delivery disarmed the details of the story, instead forcing his audience into uncomfortable confrontations with their own embarrassing memories.

That fascination with the raw truths of love and sex continued into **Different Class**, where it's seemlessly integrated into a cold hard scrutiny of both the British class system and the state of working-class Britain in the Nineties. Whereas other Britpop bands were eager to present themselves as lovable thugs, and make a virtue of boorishness, Pulp were having nothing to do with the glorification of all things yobbish. Despite Cocker's art-school background, they all came from good working-class stock.

Throughout *Different Class*, a succession of powerful, uncomprising songs – none more so than the magnificent, anthemic Underwear – kick open the bedroom doors of Britain, to expose the hypocrisy, lust and adultery that lie within. Disco 2000 and Something Changed simply ooze unrequited lust, while Pencil Skirt deals with the temptation of an illicit lover. F.E.E.L.I.N.G.C.A.L.L.E.D.L.O.V.E depicts the confusion and loss of self that comes with love, whereas Live Bed Show dwells on the seediness once that love dies. On I Spy, Jarvis heavy-breathes the words like a phone pervert who's run a mile.

The album cranks up an extra gear when it tackles the everyday experience of the lumpen proletariat. Mis-Shapes is a hymn for anyone who has been picked on, picked out or ignored, standing up for brains over brawn and individuals against the herd, while Monday Morning pokes a furred tongue at the "drunk every night and clubbing all weekend" crowd. Sorted For E's And Wizz, another single, grabbed the headlines until the papers realized this was anything but a glorification of teenagers getting messed up out in muddy fields on cold English nights, while Bar Italia (named for a real cafe in London's Soho) casts a fairly gentle eye over the fragile, small hours clientele that fall through the doors when the clubs finally close.

The album's undisputed masterpiece, however – for its perceptive lyrics, production, dynamics and venom – is Common People. If any song could ever convey to outsiders the depths of ing the sheer depths of bitterness, jealousy and resentment caused by the class system in Britain, this must be the one. Crawling with contempt, it describes a rich girl who's slumming her way through the lower orders, play-acting at poverty. The real passion and hatred in Cocker's voice grows in intensity as the song drives towards its climax; it's enough to bring a tear to the eye of any retired working-class heroes still out there. Musically too, this is Pulp's finest hour, with the rhythm section of Nick Banks and Steve Mackey providing as usual an unshakeable backing for their multi-instrumentalist colleagues.

➲ We almost chose **His'n'Hers**, Island, 1994

# 73

# Radiohead

## The Bends

Parlophone/Capitol, 1995

Thom Yorke (gtr, pno, vocals), Colin Greenwood (bass), Jon Greenwood (kbds, gtr), Ed O'Brian (gtr), Phil Selway (drums), John Matthias (strings). Caroline Lavelle (strings).

With **The Bends**, Radiohead achieved the high point of their peculiarly English, intellectual take on grunge. Renowned for a self-confidence that borders on arrogance, and a refusal to compromise – Thom Yorke once told his audience in an interview "If you're not interested, fuck you" – their reputation is founded on a finely honed sense of grievance and contempt and an acute, if dyspeptic, vision of the follies of modern life.

Although it proved responsible for turning Radiohead into a stadium-filling act, *The Bends* was written while the band were attempting to consolidate the (albeit minor) success of their debut album, *Pablo Honey* (1993). The inspiration for that album had been relatively provincial: for *The Bends*, however, they had the whole experience of the rock-star lifestyle, and in particular a US tour supporting their mentors, R.E.M., upon which to draw. A multi-talented but self-contained unit, they had developed an intense inward-looking vision, only augmented here by the addition of the string section.

Redolent of sapped strength, dissipation and even despair, *The Bends* stumbles from slowly paced sadness to mid-paced stewing anger, with occasional flashes of guitar-drenched anger. When the songs aren't declaiming about universal gloom and the futility of existence, they tend to be hinting at personal disasters and relationships gone awry; either way, they're pretty much guaranteed to appeal to a huge audience of misunderstood teenagers. Planet Telex and The Bends, for example, the two opening tracks, are big-sounding productions, bursting with huge drum sounds, urgent vocals, fear and paranoia, which if anything gain in strength by being non-specific.

Contrasting slower, gently phrased verses, highlit by little touches like tremolo piano, with crashing refrains and fiery guitar solos, Radiohead re-defined the nihilism of grunge. Opening it to outside influences, and introducing more thought-provoking lyrics, they gave it a wider dynamic, re-inventing the rock anthem in such tracks as High And Dry - an exploration of drug-tinged loneliness – and Fake Plastic Trees and Nice Dream, which set out to dissect superficial, silicone-enhanced lives.

Just, a harrowing story of home invasion and rape on the fifteenth floor, complete with "Teen Spirit" intro and tortuous dentist-drill guitar, shows how bleak and depersonalized the Radiohead vision could be. My Iron Lung and Bullet Proof...I Wish I Was draw parallels between the hermetically sealed life of the rock star, contractually obliged to keep producing, and the emotionally numbed, terminally bored audience. In Black Star – the eloquent examination of the terrible collapse of a relationship and the nervous breakdown that results – the resigned regret of the vocal contrasts wildly with the instrumentally expressed anger. Sulk, a waltz-time, enigmatic boy/girl story, glistens most when the guitar takes over mid-song, to increase the angst one more notch before the final track Street Spirit [Fade Out], all late-night urban paranoia and cold machine death, sends the audience glum and silent on its way.

It might appear surprising for such an unremittingly stark and powerful album to be dedicated to a stand-up comedian. When the comic in question is the late Bill Hicks, however, whose blackly humorous railing against injustice matched that of Radiohead line for line, it seems entirely appropriate.

⊃ We almost chose **OK Computer**, Parlophone, 1997

# 74

# The Ramones

## The Ramones

Sire, 1976

Joey Ramone (vocals), Dee Dee Ramone (bass), Johnny Ramone (gtr), Tommy Ramone (drums).

The Ramones shambled out of Queens, New York, to kick the flabby backside of rock'n'roll, and, in the process, brought the fun back into being a music-loving teenager. It would be hard to overestimate the importance of the first Ramones album, **The Ramones**; a turning point in rock music, it launched punk upon the US, established much of its musical vocabulary, and triggered a creative outpouring of magazines, record labels and bands.

Formed in early 1974, the Ramones rediscovered, during a gloriously shambolic residency at CBGBs, the raw beauty of three chords, dumb lyrics, and black leather jackets. Direct descendants of the MC5, Stooges, Dictators and New York Dolls, they cobbled together a gallery of freaks to rival the Velvet Underground's cast of Manhattan superstars. The guitar maelstrom which backed the tales of Suzy the Headbanger, Judy the Punk and Sheena the Punk-Rocker became as instantly recognizable as Chuck Berry's signature sound.

In addition to providing rock-solid primitive drumming, Tommy Ramone – Tommy Erdelyi to his school teachers – produced the album, and captured the raw Ramones essentials: no extended guitar solos, and no overdubbing after the dust settled. They stripped rock'n'roll down like a sports-chopped Harley, to an easy-to-play, power-crazed beast. Joey – tall, thin, drunk and propped up by the mike stand – had perfected his blocked-nose street-kid delivery. Johnny played his guitar like a chainsaw, while Dee Dee delivered the greatest one-note basslines known to humanity.

Played loud, with nothing longer than the epic two-minute-thirty-seven-second I Don't Wanna Go Down To The Basement, this is music to jump up and down to, pumped up with teenage lust, and pure-hearted rebellious attitude. In the desert of Little Feat's good-times boogie and the Four Seasons barbershop pop, the Ramones came like a drink of ice water. Their shock tactics extended to the lyrics – cigarette-packet sketches of child abuse, glue-sniffing and cartoon Nazi imagery – and helped divide the new-wave wheat from the old-wave chaff. Those who argued that the Ramones weren't skilled instrumentalists were never going to get the point anyway; their surly, sneering, dumb insolence, the "second verse, same as the first" idiocy, were an essential part of their freshness and appeal.

Fourteen tracks delivered in a touch over thirty minutes, *The Ramones* opens with a guitar revved up and ready to go, moving into a rallying cry of "Hey ho! Let's go!" before letting rip for two minutes of pure adrenaline. Beat On The Brat, based on a real-life incident, keeps a joyful smile on the face, despite the subject matter, which breaks into a full-on sunshine grin for Judy Is A Punk, a life story told in ninety seconds dead. There's a good deal of first-hand experience in 53rd And 3rd, too, set on New York's then-notorious street corner meat rack for male prostitutes. Dee Dee had worked there, and his confusion shines through the knife-wielding macho fantasy.

Never letting the excitement or pace falter, the album roars on through tongue-tied adolescent love stories like I Wanna Be Your Boyfriend and Listen To My Heart. With the cheeky, political spoofing on Havana Affair and Today Your Love, Tomorrow The World, and even a revived Sixties pop classic, Let's Dance, given the treatment, the Ramones created a heart-racing, pulse-enhancing classic.

⊃ We almost chose **It's Alive!**, Sire, 1979

148

# 75

# Lou Reed

## Transformer

RCA, 1972

Lou Reed (vocals, gtr, kbds), David Bowie (vocals), Ronnie Ross (sax), Herbie Flowers (bass, tuba), Mick Ronson (gtr, pno), Barry DeSouza, John Halsey, Ritchie Dharma (drums), Klaus Voormann (bass).

The appeal of Lou Reed lies in his continuing belief in love and his inability to portray it as isolated from its pitfalls and the filthy, uncaring world in which it flourishes. In 1972, almost three years after he'd put an end to the Velvet Underground, he was to all intents retired from New York's after-midnight world. Despite his Long Island isolation, however – earning a living as a typist at his father's firm – he was still working on his music, crisply documenting his acquaintances among Warhol's Manhattan demi-monde of socialites and acolytes.

The greatness of **Transformer** stems from the friction generated when Lou, the epitome of New York cool, placed himself, with understandable caution, in the Midas-like hands of his most famous imitator, South London's David Bowie. Bowie offered Reed support and a hero's welcome from the London rock scene, plus space to dabble in makeup (and some useful tips presumably) and enjoy the life of an "out" bisexual – something that had earned him electro-shock therapy back in New York State.

Vicious, sparked by an off-the-cuff remark from Warhol, typifies this contrast of light and dark, love and hate. A sex and love song, it's a campy exploration of fighting with a lover, set off by Mick Ronson's precisely distorted guitar chops. Satellite Of Love conceals jealous paranoia behind a beautifully structured, tender melody, and even Andy's Chest, full of hallucinogenic bats, bears and snakes, is a love song rounded off by orgasmic images of soldiers, diamonds, mountains all "for you".

Perfect Day – a classic subversive glam-rock opus – undergoes periodic revivals on mainstream radio as a classy, yet harmless, pop song. With its sentimental listing of activities (from Sangria in the park to a late-night movie), and lazy smoke-filled cocktail-lounge piano, it's easy to dismiss Reed's sly hint that all this bliss might come from a $10 street corner deal – until the ominous refrain, "You're going to reap just what you sow".

The more "throwaway" rock'n'roll songs are equally sugary on the outside, with bitter centres. Hangin' Round, with its crisp, dismissive character assassinations, is a full-on bitch session; Wagon Wheel, seemingly assembled from fragments of four unrelated songs, is suspended from an eerie mid-section where Lou prays "Oh Heavenly Father, I know I have sinned, but look where I've been"; and I'm So Free disguises lines like "Then we went down to Times Square, and ever since I've been hanging round there" with hand-claps and joyous whoops. Reed's claim to be "Mother Nature's son" is denied by his neon tan.

Walk On The Wild Side, the best-known track, counts as an affectionate homage to the boys, girls and undecideds of Warhol's Factory. The only song ever to enter the charts despite an overt reference to the art of the blow job, it disarms the casual listener with shuffling drums, Herbie Flowers' outstanding, sexy bass line, and the sensual sax solo from Ronnie Ross (Bowie's former sax tutor). New York Telephone Conversation, too, refers back to the gallery glitterati, while Make Up, with its jolly tuba riff backing the lyric "We're coming out, out of our closets", is a sly portrait of Warhol's characters and superstars.

Goodnight Ladies is the all-time classic "drink up and go home" song, set off here by trad-jazz, vaudeville stylings. Amid hints of the Velvets' old closing tune "After Hours", Lou swaggers off stage under a single spotlight, with a singalong suggestion – "C'mon, let's get high" – that is truly hard to resist.

➲ We almost chose **Berlin**, RCA, 1973

# 76

# R.E.M.

## Murmur

IRS, 1983

Michael Stipe (vocals), Peter Buck (gtr), Bill Berry (bass, pcn, drums), Mike Mills (bass, drums).

In an era overwhelmed by the dark and gloomy hangover from punk rock, R.E.M. put a jangle back into the guitar sound, and took US rock music back to the garage. Initially formed to play a friend's party at the University of Georgia in Athens, Georgia, the band became underground heroes long before the rest of the world caught on and banished them to the stadium-circuit ghetto. R.E.M. paid their dues in the first three years of the Eighties, hauling their equipment to play live all over the US, becoming the voice of a generation and hacking out their own distinctive sound in the process.

Their first single, Radio Free Europe, was the spark that led to the R.E.M. explosion. A driving, catchy rocker that came out on the minuscule local indie label Hib-Tone, it captured all the essential features of the band: priceless, sparkling guitar that looked back to the pure pop of the Cars, piano riffing, drums held far back, a hint of the Flamin' Groovies, and virtually incomprehensible vocals. Even when re-recorded for their debut album, **Murmur**, Stipe's voice, with its traces of Alex Chilton, and his cryptic lyrics, was muffled deep in the mix, making the album title seem entirely appropriate.

The band laid out its rich palette of ideas and influences – from the Box Tops to the Byrds – on tracks such as Pilgrimage and Laughing, with its novel bass-led introduction and happy-sad melody. Other cuts combine innocent tunes and thought-provoking, fragmented lyrics: Talk About The Passion, for example, hints that religion is just a cold, uninvolved routine for those who attend church through habit only, while the relentless repetition in We Walk makes an otherwise corny, finger-picked, Herman's-Hermits-style ditty seem sinister and oppressive.

The multi-faceted beauty of R.E.M.'s brilliant, shiny tunes is rooted in the careful assembly of timeless pop components. Essentially simple melodies are given complexity by the frequent use of false endings and re-starts. Stipe's vague, melancholy mumblings only add to the intrigue. Always inventive, yet never afraid to employ cheesy pop tricks to give a song an extra hook, R.E.M. allow the bass, guitar and voice to jostle amiably for attention. Thus the hectic West Of The Fields, bristling with straining vocals and a call-and-response chorus, or the aggressive 9-9, whose clashing guitar and drum motif harks back to the Gang Of Four, moving away from straight pop music with chanted vocals and oblique lyrics (only "conversation fear", the final two words, are totally clear).

The band excel at urgent, stripped-down slices of Americana such as Catapult – sounding like the Jam, with Buck's Rickenbacker guitar on overdrive, and precision harmonic vocals – and the epic Sitting Still. Both capture R.E.M. at their antsy-adolescent best: rushing, driving, gotta-get-out bursts of excitement.

As *Murmur* proves, R.E.M. were brimming over with ideas from the moment they first entered the recording studio. Darker than powerpop, but sharing its energy, confidence and excitement, their music had a pop sensibility that came as a welcome alternative to the then-prevailing hardcore scene. Voted best of the year by *Rolling Stone*, *Murmur* was a remarkable achievement, which sounds as fresh today as it did on release. R.E.M. did more with the basic "guitars, vocals and drums" formula than any band since the Beatles; they went on, of course, to world domination, but they never surpassed their debut.

➲ We almost chose **Automatic For The People**, Warner, 1992

# 77

# Rolling Stones

## Exile On Main Street

Rolling Stones Records, 1972

Mick Jagger (gtr, harp, kbds, vocals), Keith Richards (gtr, kbds, vocals), Mick Taylor (gtr, vocals), Bill Wyman (synth, bass, kbds), Charlie Watts (drums), Ian Stewart (kbds), Billy Preston (kbds), Nicky Hopkins (kbds), Jim Price (kbds, horns), Jimmy Miller (pcn), Bobby Keys (horn, sax), Jim Miller (pcn), Dr John (vocals).

**Exile On Main Street** is a late-night album from the darkside, recorded after hours by musicians who saw bourbon and cigarettes as food, and had a well-known taste for more illicit pleasures. The Rolling Stones sound was never dirtier, characterized by Mick's slurriest delivery and Keef's sloppiest riffing, both of them leaning on Charlie's drumming and Bill's resigned bass for advice and support. A current of need runs through the vocals, either explicit in the lyrics, or implicit in their delivery. It's all informed by "junkie chic", certainly, but thanks to the emotional turbulence and epic-level abuse of drugs and alcohol that went on within the Stones entourage, there's also plenty of first-hand input. Certain albums become associated with certain drugs; Motorhead's first album, for example, yells "amphetamine sulphate", while on Fleetwood Mac's *Rumours* you can almost hear the gold-plated razor blades tinkling the coke across the mirrors deep down in the mix. *Exile On Main Street*, by contrast, reeks of heroin and expensive whisky.

An air of world-weary defiance permeates the entire album – witness "Sunshine bores the daylights out of me"; "You gotta scrape the shit right off your shoes"; and "You're gonna be the death of me" – as it unmistakably celebrates the needle'n'spoon lifestyle. The narcotic cruise of Tumbling Dice, with its swaggering guitar vamp and unfiltered cigarette stuck jauntily into the side of its grin, is Keef's crowning moment of decadence. That said, credit should be given for the disturbingly honest flipside to all this powdered fun and games, as displayed in the cold turkey, morning light of Ventilator Blues and Loving Cup, full of pain and strung-out begging for relief.

With its jaded, sleazy brass section *Exile* works perfectly well as a straightforward louche rock album; the New York Dolls were doing much the same kind of act at the time, despite being a generation younger. However, it's repeatedly jolted into greatness by unforgettable touches like Mick's frantic desire to have a good time in Rip This Joint, where he sounds scared that the party will happen without him.

The good times crash amid the muffled vocals and muddy piano of Just Wanna See His Face. Easily the most disturbing track on the album, it hints of powerfully affecting experiments with the occult, and leaves a nasty aftertaste of pain, sex, blood and death. The Stones excelled at adding the perfect final ingredient to their gripping urban dramas. Casino Boogie ends with a delicious cool sax break from Bobby Keys; the junkie whine of Torn And Frayed is underlined by the poignant pedal steel of Al Perkins; and the tormented harp on Stop Breaking Down beautifully sets off Mick Taylor's best guitar work.

Keef's magnificently sincere Happy, written in a period of relative sobriety, may not settle the debates as to who was the true "leader" of the band, but he kept this one for himself. Even if he rarely approaches such pure joy these days, it remains a highlights of the Stones' live appearances. Another beautiful love song, betrayed by its dated phrasing, is Black Angel; this track-crossing ode to "the exotic" owes more to Van Morrison than to the dubious racial attitudes of their own "Brown Sugar".

Epic, personal, sloppy and flawless, *Exile On Main Street* remains the Rolling Stones' collective high.

➲ We almost chose **Beggars Banquet**, London, 1968

# 78

# Roxy Music

## For Your Pleasure

EG, 1973

Bryan Ferry (vocals, kbds), Brian Eno (synth, kbds, tape), Phil Manzanera (gtr), Andy MacKay (oboe, sax), John Porter (bass), Paul Thompson (drums).

"There's a new sensation / a fabulous creation / a danceable solution / to teenage revolution". Thus Roxy Music arrogantly stated their case in the opening lines of **For Your Pleasure**, their second, breakthrough album. Yes, it was a sensationally new sound, sort of Cole Porter meets Little Richard meets Miles Davis. But that doesn't begin to describe Brian Eno's eerie sonic landscapes, Phil Manzanera's quicksilver guitar runs, Andy Mackay's otherworldly sax or even Anthony Price's designer-camp image for the band. And, of course, it doesn't encompass the key element of Roxy's vision – Bryan Ferry's mannered cool. Too intellectual for glam, too kitsch for prog-rock, it had a louche charm all of its own.

Ferry, who came from a mining community in northeast England, dabbled in pop-art experimentalism at art college, and tried his hand as a ceramics teacher, before he came up with the Roxy Music concept. Not until he auditioned to replace Greg Lake in King Crimson did the music industry become alerted to his talents. Signed to Island, Roxy were an immediate success. Their first single, "Virginia Plain" – two-and-a-half minutes of clever wordplay, chic rock'n'roll, and art-school romanticism, perversely not included on their debut album – shot up the UK charts. All mascara, Brylcreem, brothel-creepers and sequins, Ferry became a teenage pin-up. Another left-field hit,

"Pyjamarama", consolidated Roxy's reputation in the UK, although America failed to warm to their charms.

The Roxy Music sound crystallized on 1973's *For Your Pleasure* – "the one", said Ferry, "that captured what I wanted to do most clearly". Here was an album that mixed the primitive rock 'n' roll of Do The Strand and Editions Of You with the dark funk of The Bogus Man and the ethereal, avant-garde futurism of For Your Pleasure itself. All was peppered with Ferry's sharp irony, and filtered through Eno's tape machines to sound as though it came from another planet. And then there was Ferry's masterpiece, In Every Dreamhome A Heartache, which distilled his recurrent themes of loneliness, melancholia and obsession into a haunting tale of sex-doll fixation. Ferry's psychotic delivery and sick humour ("I blew up your body / but you blew my mind") are chilling, but Manzanera's swirling guitars at the song's climax are what take us to the very heart of his darkness.

As the band's popularity grew, Eno's white-noise experimentalism and outrageous dress sense began to make him the focus of attention. That inevitably led to ego conflicts with Ferry, and Eno left after *For Your Pleasure*. Make no mistake, it was Ferry's album, but with Eno's departure the fizz went out of Roxy. Each subsequent album became less interesting, to the point where the Roxy Music of the Eighties produced little more than wallpaper music. Ferry also intermittently developed his lounge-lizard persona on a number of patchy solo albums, of which only 1978's accomplished *Bride Stripped Bare* really hit the spot, and then at a time when most fans were too preoccupied to notice. For a man once considered as a rock visionary, his fall has been dramatic, while Brian Eno, ambient svengali and producer of Talking Heads, Bowie and U2, has had the last laugh.

*For Your Pleasure* is an album that looks back as well as forward. Its exotic cover image, of a stilettoed Amanda Lear leading her pet panther to a pink Cadillac chauffeured by Ferry, promises a lush hedonism, quite at odds with the denim-and-earnestness approach so prevalent in the early Seventies. It delivers.

➲ We almost chose **Roxy Music**, EG, 1972

# 79

# The Sex Pistols

## Never Mind The Bollocks, Here's The Sex Pistols

Virgin, 1977

John Lydon (vocals), Steve Jones (bass, gtr), Paul Cook (drums), Glen Matlock (bass), Sid Vicious (bass, vocals).

Even twenty-odd years down the line, it's hard not to let the hype and the legend obscure the fact that **Never Mind The Bollocks, Here's The Sex Pistols** is, undeniably, a great rock album. With hindsight, its traditional rock influences are obvious – the yobbish, sub-Faces guitar chords, the elegant but simple basslines lifted straight from the Jon Entwistle school, and the stripped-down drumming that owed its soul to the Detroit garage bands. In fact, in retrospect, there's little iconoclastic about the music at all; it's just a little faster in places, with more fuzz and distortion than usual. Then, suddenly, that voice puts everything else in the shade, and the reason for all the fuss becomes clear.

Jones, Cook and Matlock – with a little help from the session men – recorded a dozen tracks, only to have them beaten, throttled and hidden away behind the voice of Johnny Rotten, the most powerful and instantly recognizable noise in punk rock. Opening with marching feet, martial drums and a powerchord, Holidays In The Sun makes clear the intent to take no prisoners. Bodies, next, is a full-speed, very personal, grief-turned-to-anger rant, despite its football-terrace chorus. No Feelings, by comparison, has a cheeky, villainous swagger. Reminiscent of early Who mod-anthems, the lyrics have a detached amphetamine sheen and "no feelings, for anybody else". Liar was a short sharp burst of schoolyard petulance, twitching with jerking, impotent rage. Johnny Rotten was never going to kick anyone's ass, but his sarcasm and contempt could strip steel plate.

The Sex Pistols had a gift for singalongs, and God Save The Queen became a rallying cry. As a single, it had battered its way to the top of the UK charts against a background of strikes at the pressing plants, media outrage and political rhetoric, and was welcomed as an alternative national anthem for all those alienated by the fervent monarchism of that jubilee year. It's the epitome of punk rock: snotty and contemptuous, defiant, frantic for change yet totally uninterested in providing solutions. It starts with an earthquake, builds to a climax, and even ends with a chant of "no future". Problems and Seventeen, further torrents of paranoid disillusionment, lead into Anarchy In The UK, the first and best punk anthem in the world, full of wonderful teenage nihilism and speed-fed confidence.

Rotten once proclaimed that "Love is three minutes of squelching noises"; strange then, the emotional intensity of Submission, a hymn to cunnilingus laid over guitar licks lifted from the Who's "Can't Explain". Best move on to Pretty Vacant, with its stunning opening riff and fantastic juxtaposition of words; the Pistols were far from pretty, and nowhere near as vacant as they made out.

As a blatant sneer at Johnny Thunders, who'd toured the UK with the Sex Pistols as part of the Heartbreakers, New York caused a major spat between the British and US schools of punk. Insulting Thunders' look, his old band the New York Dolls, and, perhaps most tellingly, his dependence on narcotics, the song has Rotten destroying one of his major influences – a favour Thunders paid back in spades with his riposte "London Boys".

The album closes with the gleeful taunting of EMI, a company that had briefly been home to the band. A throwaway track, it nonetheless has all the elements that made the Pistols great: the posturing, the powerchords, and the incandescent ranting.

⮞ The Pistols only recorded one album

# 80

# Jane Siberry

## When I Was A Boy

Reprise, 1993

Jane Siberry (vocals, gtr, kbds), Brian Eno (synth, producer), Michael Brook (gtr, producer), Teddy Borowiecki (pno), Erdal Kizilgay (pno), Anne Bourne (strings), Ben Mink (strings), k. d. lang (vocals), James West (kbds, gtr), Bryant Didier (bass), John Switzer (bass), Glenn Milchem (drums), James Pinker (drums).

An ultra-skilled and incomparably expressive singer, Jane Siberry ranks among the most original and inventive artists of the last two decades. Even today, her work displays the operatic and classical influences she absorbed in childhood, as her vocals swerve from intimate whispered confessions to abstract episodes of sheer wordless colour and texture.

When Siberry first came to public attention, with the release in 1981 of *Jane Siberry*, her music was already full of eccentrically phrased self-examination. Her cinematic, narrative style continued to develop throughout the Eighties, particularly on her third album, *The Speckless Sky*, and follow-up *The Walking*. This latter, her major-label debut, was the recording that broke her to a devoted but distressingly small international audience.

After the more commercial direction of 1989's *Bound By Beauty* proved fruitless, Siberry took three years to explore new musical territory before signing up Brian Eno – himself a fan – to produce and contribute to **When I Was A Boy**. Her return to the outer limits, it remains her greatest piece of work.

The album opens with Temple, a throbbing, lust-filled celebration of desire (with a wicked, glint-in-the-eye "mmmm . . . gimme" line used as part of the percussive backing), all unstoppable drums and Frippertronics guitar effects. Siberry moves away from such earthly notions in Calling All Angels, a list of holy-sounding names that slowly ascends to a pure and noble peak of heavenly harmonies (featuring guest vocalist k. d. lang). She then leaves the real world altogether for an elegant meditation on love and its ending in Love Is Everything – whose gentle piano backing and lyrical style echo Joni Mitchell's mid-Seventies work – and Sail Across The Water, where the stronger rock influences, and heavy dash of Eno, look back to Laurie Anderson.

However, *When I Was A Boy* is at its most stunning during the less conventional tracks. Sweet Incarnadine, edited down from a twenty-minute improvisation, combines a celebratory, chaste arrangement with phrasing on the verge of ecstatic, and lyrics that hint at sexual passion. The true peak is The Vigil, searingly informed by the recent death of Siberry's father. A work of harrowing grandeur, it explores both religion and love, framed in the intimate context of drifting asleep in a chair while watching over the body of a loved one. Her singing suggests not only loss but also a strange contentment, with a slow-heartbeat percussion to signal that all is well, all is ultimately at peace. Siberry lets loose with some of her boldest vocal experiments – even changing the scene, dreamlike, to images of hiding in the city and sleeping on a deserted beach – yet retains the necessary perfect dignity throughout, never for an instant relaxing her control.

A marvellous recording for the tender and the lonely, heart-broken lovers and self-pitying drunks, *When I Was A Boy* plummets from the peaks of joy to the deepest despair. The faultless production and multiple perspectives of many of the songs (reminiscent of Patti Smith at her most incisive) only adds to the sharpness of the pain. Moving away from her occasional pop, and even dance, dalliances, Siberry takes the best of art-rock, strips away any hint of self-indulgence, and verges at times towards ambient music. There comes a time in every life when only an album of such unutterable sadness will do.

➲ We almost chose **Bound By The Beauty**, Reprise, 1989

# 81

# Sleater-Kinney

## Call The Doctor

Matador/Chainsaw Records, 1996

Corin Tucker (gtr, vocals, drums), Carrie Kinney, originally Carrie Brownstein (gtr, vocals), Lora Macfarlane (drums).

Emerging from the creative musical stew of the far northwestern USA, home to the Riot Grrrl movement, Sleater-Kinney took their name from a road in Olympia (Washington State) and set about constructing gutsy, emotive songs drenched in political commitment and the resolve to instigate change. The band gave a new female voice to punk rock and, dispensing with the traditional bass guitar, made a new sound to accompany it. Tipping a hat to grunge as well as to old-school punk, they created a strong, pure and simple rock-'n'roll sound that acknowledged acts as diverse as the Slits and Bikini Kill without slavishly following anybody.

**Call The Doctor**, their second album, built on the successful reception awarded their raw, self-titled debut. Recorded in 24 hours spread over two weeks, and released on locally based queercore label Chainsaw in 1995, *Call The Doctor* broke them to a wider international audience. The band's incisive and hardcore – if po-faced – dissections of gender and sexual inequality, and a rampant materialist state, were complemented by magnificent rock'n'roll concepts such as I Want To Be Your Joey Ramone (a slow riffing, mash note with a gorgeous, passionate refrain), and the two-word chorus to I'm Not Waiting ("honeybabysweetnessdarlingimyourlittlegirl" and "yourwordsarestickystupidrunningdownmyleg"). Extra texture came through

Macfarlane and Brownstein's increased vocal contributions, and their irresistible streetwise harmonies.

From the start, the album aims to put the skids under political inertia. Call The Doctor itself captures the band's urgent, chiming, guitar-heavy punk rock with a blend of the Gang Of Four's "5.45" riff and individual words, delivered with a solid emphasis that staples them into place. At times, as in Hubcap, My Stuff and closing track Heart Attack, brooding guitars and sheets of percussion back up lyrics so fragmented as to seem coded, reminiscent of, if less introspective than, Throwing Muses or PJ Harvey's early material. Elsewhere, for example on Little Mouth and the Buzzcocks-meets-the-Ronettes masterpiece Stay Where You Are – the standout track on an album packed with cool cuts – vintage punk-rock values come to the fore.

Good Things (a melodic, Flamin' Groovies-style cruising groove) reveals the obsession at the end of love through plaintive simple, direct lyrics ("Why do good things never want to stay?") while Taking Me Home lurches wildly round in distorted, sleaze-waltz time. In both Taste Test and "I'm Not Waiting", Tucker delivers far from explicit sex-life lyrics in a voice straining for attention behind frenetic chord thrashes. Sleater-Kinney never need to search hard for a target, and every target gets a song. Whatever the format, the music oozes sincerity and commitment, using righteous anger and integrity to blitz stale conformity and urge rebellion.

Activists with more to offer than mere shouting riot grrrl diatribes, Sleater-Kinney are among the most important musicians of the Nineties. They make music with a swaggering, fearsome intensity that's prepared, if necessary, to trade punches: a sound that you can't push around. For *Dig Me Out*, their 1997 album, Macfarlane was replaced by Janet Weiss, but the band played on, poking their collective head over the rim of the indie underworld. The more commercially aware tone of their most recent release, *The Hot Rock*, promises to introduce them to the mainstream, but with no sell-out, and no disappointments either.

⮕ We almost chose **The Hot Rock**, Kill Rock Stars, 1999

# 82

# Patti Smith

## Horses

Arista, 1975

Patti Smith (gtr, vocals), Ivan Kral (bass, gtr, kbds), Richard Sohl (pno), Jay Dee Daugherty (drums), Lenny Kaye (bass, gtr), Tom Verlaine (gtr), Allen Lanier (gtr, kbds), John Cale (bass, producer).

As a product of the Richard Hell–Tom Verlaine–Television music scene, based at New York's CBGB club, Patti Smith should have been pretentious beyond bearing. In fact, with her gritty New Jersey background and flair for social documentary, she lapped up the work of romantic anti-heroes from Rimbaud to Baudelaire, Jim Morrison to Jimi Hendrix, added a whirl of Burroughs-esque obsession, and created, in **Horses**, one of the most important albums of the Seventies. Echoing the dead-eyed reportage of Lou Reed, she incorporated industrial-strength doses of poetry and jazz into her pounding, insistent and downright thrilling rock manifesto.

The opening cut of *Horses*, Gloria: In Excelsis Deo, kicks off with the majestic statement that "Jesus died for somebody's sins but not mine". Smith then completely subverts, reclaims and re-invents female lust with her re-interpretation of the Them classic "Gloria". A stripped-down riff allows her room to rap about a "sweet young thing humping on the parking meter", as the song slowly builds to a screaming, full-on, rock'n'roll climax.

Smith's casual references to homosexual love, also evident in the next track, Redondo Beach, were immensely bold for the time. The narrative of a girlfriend's suicide, set in what was then *the* dyke resort, is recounted in flat, emotionally neutral words that, by their sheer lack of feeling, suggest somebody too wracked by grief to be able to accept the loss. The tragedy is only emphasized by the white reggae bounce of the tune.

Throughout Horses, science-fiction images and visionary trips to other worlds merge with disturbing stream-of-consciousness babbling, sometimes openly sexual. Birdland moves from the monotonous wail of an alien yearning to go home to scenes of running through fields, while the apocalyptic visions of Kimberley (named for Patti's sister) are drawn from Smith's religious upbringing, and verge on speaking in tongues. On Break It Up, Tom Verlaine's swooping guitar backs the chest-beating Smith through visions of "the boy" until the catharsis of "I ripped my skin open and then I broke through".

On Free Money, by contrast, it's the down-to-earth, blue-collar New Jersey native talking. The everyday dream of any poor person, the song elevates cash to the level where it can answer all questions, solve all problems, and even represent love.

The unquestioned standout on Horses, however, is the epic Land. Divided into three distinct sections, it combines emotionless narrative and free-expression poetic explosions into a compelling tale of sex and death. The first part, "Horses", reintroduces "the boy" as homosexual rapist. With an insistent fuck-rhythm, Smith recites splintered imagery to create a tale of conquest, surrender and fighting back – reminiscent of Last Exit To Brooklyn – that detonates into the second part, an ecstatic, erotic version of "Land Of A Thousand Dances". Here, when Patti asks "Do you know how to pony?", she hints at more than a dance step. Demanding "Do you like it like that?", she's not asking for comment on her dance technique.

Equally explicit sexual imagery dominates the horse-populated third section "La Mer(de)", in which scenes come in waves like the Arabian stallions it describes. Smith's triple-tracked vocals reveal "I felt his hand on my knee", and "I felt him hardening in my hand", before she cools off, slows down, and comes full circle, referring back to Gloria, humping on a parking meter.

➲ We almost chose **Easter**, Arista, 1978

# 83

# The Smiths

## Hatful of Hollow

Rough Trade, 1984; reissued Warner, 1984

Steven Morrissey (vocals), Johnny Marr (gtr, harmonica, mandolin), Andy Rourke (bass), Mike Joyce (drums).

Though assembled from B-sides and early radio sessions, the **Hatful of Hollow** compilation displays the most influential British band of the Eighties during its most creative two years. Before drug abuse and ego inflation killed the Smiths, they created some of the most original music in the history of rock, and completely re-defined "indie" music in the UK. Morrissey had been on the verges of the music scene since he tried to start a British chapter of the New York Dolls' fan club back in the Seventies. Not until the bedroom lyricist hooked up with guitar-genius Marr, however, did he finally move into public view.

Morrissey and Marr chose a bluff, no-nonsense name for the Smiths to balance the complex beauty of their music, and picked up sterling support from Joyce and Rourke. In May 1983, when they made the first of the recordings here, they had been together as a band for just eight months, of which six had been spent touring the UK. While it's always tempting to see lyrics as autobiographical, Morrissey's flamboyant, frankly menacing stage persona seemed to have little in common with the sensitive loners portrayed in his songs. Even so, although he claimed to be living an asexual existence, a theme of hidden shame, guilt and schoolboy fumbling runs through the band's early work; to quote the man himself, "the hills are alive with celibate lies".

Immediate public acclaim resulted in a deal with Rough Trade, and a single, Hand In Glove, that combined good old-fashioned rock'n'roll arrogance ("The sun shines out of our behinds") with a story of love unashamed. Similar topics reappear in the rain-drenched William, It Was Really Nothing, Still Ill ("England is mine and it owes me a living"), and Accept Yourself (on which Morrissey, at his most Scott Walker-ish, mourns how time has slipped through his fingers).

There was genuine depth and variety to the Smiths. Back To The Old House and Please, Please, Please, Let Me Get What I Want, for example, convey a touching sadness. How Soon Is Now sees them indulge in a little drugged-up introspection, a prelude to the numbness of This Night Has Opened My Eyes, describing the disposal of an unwanted baby wrapped in newspaper. The wicked glint in the band's collective eye surfaces on the rockabilly-tinged What Difference Does It Make, on which seedy, groping mischief turns nasty. The shame of "Now you know the truth about me you won't see me any more" is reprised in These Things Take Time.

This Charming Man deals with the dynamics of power in a rich-meets-poor casual sexual encounter, illustrated with images of leather car upholstery and lyrics like "A jumped up pantry boy who never knew his place", lifted from Anthony Shaffer's film Sleuth. Handsome Devil looks at a more sinister balance of power, a schoolmaster's lust for his charges, while Girl Afraid takes a look at emotionally crippled teenagers, equally scared of commitment and rejection. The standout on an album filled with excellent cuts, however, is Reel Around The Fountain, a romantic, wistful tale of drunken seduction gently deflated through its hilariously incongruous lyrics and vocal style.

Ironically, the Smiths were doomed by their commitment to Rough Trade, who couldn't manufacture enough records to keep them at the top of the charts; the resultant arguments led to their splitting up. However, they set new standards for songwriting, and re-opened the record stores to acts on smaller labels.

➲ We almost chose **The Queen Is Dead**, Warner, 1986

# 84

# Sonic Youth

## Daydream Nation

Blast First/Enigma, 1988

Thurston Moore (gtr, vocals), Lee Ranaldo (gtr, vocals), Kim Gordon (bass, vocals),
Steve Shelley (drums).

For all of their sex-equals-madness-equals-death shtick, and their castration of the power-pleasure principle of rock, Sonic Youth were, above all, one of the best-sounding rock bands ever. At their best, the No Wave guitar overtones accumulated into slow-burning surges of overwhelming sound that were every bit as liberating as anything summoned up by Hendrix, Clapton, or any other mainstream guitar hero you care to mention. On **Daydream Nation**, those famous guitar tunings conjured epiphany, obliteration and ecstasy out of chaos and insanity more effectively than anywhere else in the Sonic Youth canon.

While punk had recognized that blues-based rock had been bled dry, and tried to tear down its walls, Sonic Youth actually proposed something else to take its place. Axemen Thurston Moore and Lee Ranaldo had both participated in avant-garde composer Glenn Branca's guitar symphonies at the start of the Eighties, and they attempted to re-cast his vision of droning, extraordinarily loud guitar amplification within the parameters of the outcast aggression of punk rock. Making their high-wire act across the art/rock divide even more perilous were Moore and bassist Kim Gordon's obsessions with bad sex, Richard Kern movies, Charles Manson, Raymond Pettibon paintings, and other objects of underground-New-York-art-death-drive-porn fascination. What rescued Sonic Youth from an eternity in the Re/Search ghetto, however, was *that* guitar sound, which became to alternative rock what Keith Richards' riffage was to the Sixties and Seventies.

On *Daydream Nation*, Sonic Youth's art-house deadpan was transcended by music as galvanizing, motorvational, and monolithic as anything the Stones ever recorded. Whereas before you'd always noticed the guitars, here it was the groove that immediately grabbed your attention. Of course, the guitars were still present and correct, it's just that now they fused with Steve Shelley's drums to create the kind of total release that Gordon and Moore's characters always craved. Beginning as a *VU*-style urban jingle-jangle, complete with a Mo Tucker mallet beat, The Sprawl ended with a psychedelic six-string panorama that lived up both to its title and to Gordon's tale of self-annihilation through debasement. Rain King had a ZZ Top power riff, while Teen Age Riot and Silver Rocket were two of the best rock'n'roll songs that the alterna-nation would produce. Elsewhere, noise and drive combined to create the sensation of physical, and not merely mental, abandon.

While the lyrics mixed metaphors and changed perspectives so often as to be intelligible only to the most committed surrealist, catchphrases stood out like battle cries: "You're so soft, you make me hard", "It takes a teenage riot to get me out of bed", "You're never gonna stop all the teenage leather", "Your city is a wonder town", "A daydreaming daze in a daydream nation", and "It's total trash". Married to the most optimistic music of their career, Lee Ranaldo's stories of wide-eyed acid casualties looking for satori, Gordon's twisted groupie fantasies, and Moore's fuck-up narratives stopped reading like the Larry Clark-esque, high-brow exploitation scenarios of old, and achieved a kind of mythopoeic grandeur that made Sonic Youth the elder statesmen of alternative rock. Alongside the Pixies' *Surfer Rosa*, the neurosis anthems of *Daydream Nation* were what made it possible for American punk rock to attain Nirvana.

➲ We almost chose **Goo**, GDC, 1990

# 85

# Spiritualized

## Ladies And Gentlemen
## We Are Floating In Space

Dedicated, 1997

Spaceman Jason Pierce (vocals, gtr, kbds, pno), Kate Radley (kbds, pno, vocals), Sean Cook (bass, harmonica), Damon Reece (drums, pcn), Dr John (vocals, pno), London Gospel Community Choir.

Having risen from the ashes of trance-master duo Spacemen 3, Jason Pierce's Spiritualized has developed a spacious, lethargic sound in which moods are extended, and instrumentals are taken to extremes. A powerful combination of droning Velvet-Underground riffing and gently trippy rambling, boosted with snatches of sparkling brass and sweeping orchestral flourishes, the whole production is used to convey the kind of "narcotic psychedelia" that makes **Ladies And Gentlemen We Are Floating In Space** the Nineties' most overtly pro-hard-drug album.

Spiritualized has always relished its wasted "sunglasses after dark" image, but on *Ladies And Gentlemen . . .* they put together a showreel for drug abuse. Music of stupendous atmosphere and beauty, composed with the hardcore stoner in mind, is topped by blissed-out, barely-able-to-function vocals. At times verging on structureless ambience, at others swerving into oncoming traffic with powerful riff-driven rock rhythms, Spiritualized prove once and for all that the drugs do indeed work.

The most effective tracks here are the most blatantly opiated. Ladies And Gentlemen . . . itself, the opener, starts with a stumbling announcement from an over-medicated "space-hostess", which leads into a childlike "round", a "Frere Jacques" for the narcotically inclined. I Think I'm In Love deals with the absence of desire that comes with a well-developed habit ("I feel the warmth of the sun in the room, I don't care about you"). The song features restrained keyboards, gentle bass and a distorted guitar line before the chanted vocals appear, then comes to a halt before a beatier call-and-response section. Lines like "I think I'm in love / Probably just hungry" destroy any lingering notion of romance. On Cool Waves, rasping vocals are laid out on a bed of string-effect keyboards and a narco-lullaby chorus. The even slower Stay With Me drifts for a long airy minute of synth swoops, slide guitar and bare hints of bass, before Jason finally manages to gasp "Oh Babe" and open the singing.

Home Of The Brave and Cop Shoot Cop – each word is a verb, signifying the vicious circle of the junkie life – could scarcely be more explicit. The former proclaims "Sometimes have my breakfast straight of the mirror", while on the latter the production allows Pierce's voice to slip away as the band fades, in an effective representation of the rush that comes when the tourniquet is let go, before it blends seamlessly into a crazy, instrumental continuation, The Individual. The nightclub-jazzy, bluesy final track states baldly "There's a hole in my arm where all the money goes".

Come Together, a prime slice of trance-rock, is the most obvious Spacemen 3-style piece, with its chanted vocals reminiscent of early Hawkwind, and a guitar/harmonica freakout held together only by the best efforts of the brass and rhythm sections. Electricity, on the other hand, is a fuzz-guitar powered garage rocker straight from the Sixties. Elsewhere, as in No God Only Religion, the band is reminiscent of Syd Barrett's Pink Floyd as it explores free-rock instrumental, while the arrangement and confessional vocals of the ballad Broken Heart suggest Robert Wyatt. All Of My Thoughts contrasts violent, loud instrumentals and twinkling piano-haunted verses with church organ touches and dreamy half-asleep vocals.

➲ We almost chose **Lazer Guided Melodies**, Dedicated, 1992

# 86

# Steely Dan

## Pretzel Logic

ABC, 1974; MCA, 1985

Walter Becker (bass, gtr), Donald Fagen (vocals, kbds), Denny Dias (gtr), Jeff "Skunk" Baxter (pedal steel gtr), Jim Hodder (drums).

A showcase of impeccable workmanship and unmatched songcraft, **Pretzel Logic** ranks among the most influential American recordings of the Seventies. Steely Dan were assembled by Donald Fagen and Walter Becker, who worked as staff writers for ABC-Dunhill records and had developed an almost instinctive understanding of one another, to play the more satisfying, adult music that they put together in their free time. Complete sound obsessives, they brought a knowing East Coast realism to a Los Angeles scene dominated by the mediocre.

Named for a sex aid made famous in William Burroughs' *Naked Lunch*, Steely Dan scored an instant hit with critics and public alike with their first release in 1973, *Can't Buy A Thrill*. By the time they recorded *Pretzel Logic*, their third album, their sound had been honed through extensive touring as a five-piece band. Steely Dan were now able to treat the studio as their playground, summoning top session men – such as the famous "Skunk" Baxter who makes such a vital contribution to the sound of this album – from around the world in their quest to obtain the precise sounds they could hear in their heads. In fact, this was their true creative peak; Fagen and Becker soon withdrew to the studio altogether, happy to quit touring, and relied on hired-in help for their subsequent albums. As yet untouched by the substance abuse, ego clashes and despondency that were to come, *Pretzel Logic*'s combination of beautifully constructed and executed music with perceptive, cynical portrayals of the modern world resulted in pop music of lasting appeal.

Fagen's world-weary, resigned sneer came into its own on bitter portraits such as the hit single Rikki Don't Lose That Number. Framed with restrained piano and drum riffs and gorgeous vocal harmonies, the vague lyrics hint that Rikki has turned her back on his past and might later regret it. The more direct Charlie Freak – a frank short story of drug abuse, stolen goods and backstreet overdoses – relies on a pattern of imposing piano chords, endlessly repeated, to support Fagen's singsong delivery. The vitriol so evident in his whining depiction of small-minded bigots in Barrytown mellows to a resigned regret in Monkey In Your Soul and Through With Buzz, which say goodbye to a lover in trouble and a friend with a problem respectively. He shines in the more positive Any Major Dude Will Tell You, with its gentle acoustic guitar and piano melody, and the boastful, rocking groove of Parker's Band.

Always consummate musicians, the band added jazz and influences to their already-broad palette on *Pretzel Logic*. Solos throughout are neatly crafted, lending insight and charm to the multi-layered lyrics. Virtuoso moments include the respectful reappraisal of Duke Ellington's East St Louis Toodle-Oo, on which Fagen gets to grandstand on keyboards while Becker plays guitar through a vocoder, and the urban, blue-eyed soul of Night By Night. Pretzel Logic itself is a slow-funking keyboard groove, a prime cut of urban blues with a tense, prowling guitar solo and urgent strident brass touches, while With A Gun, a portrait of small-time, store-robbing, urban street hoodlums, is essentially a country-folk number. Elsewhere there's lightning-fast guitar heroism on "Parker's Band", neurotic piano on "Charlie Freak", brassy sleaze-funk on "Monkey In Your Soul", and sublime strings and playful changes of pace on "Through With Buzz".

⮞ We almost chose **Can't Buy A Thrill**, ABC, 1973

# 87

# The Stone Roses

## The Stone Roses

Silvertone, 1989

Ian Brown (vocals), Gary "Mani" Mounfield (bass), Alan "Reni" Wren (drums, vocals), John Squire (gtr, paintings).

Having played together since 1984, when they were formed by ex-schoolmates Squire and Brown, the Stone Roses had by the end of the Eighties acquired the experience to create a swaggering star-making album that would set them far above their contemporaries. Cool, self-assured, and able to lean on the solid rhythm section of Reni's drumming and Mini's white-funk bass, the Roses signed to indie label Silvertone. Released at the peak of the "Madchester" scene, **The Stone Roses** stayed in the charts for eleven months.

Masters of the groove after their long apprenticeship at numberless warehouse gigs, the Roses' grounding in Squire's art-school attitudes contrasted sharply with the low-rent hedonism of the Happy Mondays. Drawing on past psychedelic masters like the Byrds and Love, their songs made frequent reference to a non-specific "she", a provider of guidance and advice, who was utterly alien to the cruder female characterizations of Shaun Ryder and his pals.

With its blend of swirling, oceanic guitar effects and direct, arrogant lyrics, I Wanna Be Adored effectively sums up the appeal of the Stone Roses. Self-contained and exquisite, the track comprises a single verse, itself based on just two phrases, but builds into a five-minute symphony. She Bangs The Drums, Waterfall, and Don't Stop skip along on a rush of sparkling crystal guitar and shine with a speedy mod sensibility. Squire's elegant, restrained guitar work leaves plenty of room for inspiring lyrics like "kiss me where the sun don't shine" to grow from abuse into cheeky mischief. The last of these three tracks – essentially the second played backwards – is an ecstasy-driven, Beatles-like studio experiment, with the giveaway blissed-out lyric "Don't stop, isn't it funny how you shine".

If the Clash had ever taken E, then Bye Bye Badman could well have been the result. A beautiful, Byrds-esque spacey guitar riff chugs merrily along while Brown slips us delicately subversive singalong lyrics full of bile ("I'm throwing stones at you and I want you black and blue"). Tripping in the middle of a riot, the Roses nail their scally colours to the mast, following up with the elegantly anti-monarchist Elizabeth My Dear – a spoof of "Scarborough Fair", as bitter as Elvis Costello's most scathing pieces – declaring beyond doubt which side of the barricades they were to be found on. This air of spiteful insurrection is reprised later in Shoot You Down, where a sly jazzy introduction distracts attention from the venom in the two funky verses.

The album's purest love song, (Song For My) Sugar Spun Sister, glistens with vaguely salacious lyrics, but the warm glow endures only as far as the gloomy opening of Made Of Stone, a darkside number featuring the chirpy "whistling in the dark" refrain of "Are you all alone? Are you made of stone?".

*The Stone Roses* closes with two tracks of heart-bursting optimism and joy. This Is The One encapsulates all the beaming smiles and empathy that comes from a big hit of your favourite poison, be it brandy or barbiturates, with none of the sleazy hangover. Swelling from a reverential bassline, it adds guitars in a musical representation of the best rush ever, and ends with the epiphany of "This is the one she's been waiting for". I Am The Resurrection is a blast of frozen mod arrogance with a glint of steel in its street-perfect slangy phrasing ("Stone me, why can't you see?"; "You bring me down"; and "I wish you'd learn") wrapped in a triumphal uplifting song.

➲ We almost chose **Turns Into Stone**, Silvertone, 1992

# 88

# The Stooges

## The Stooges

Elektra/Asylum, 1969

Iggy Pop (vocals), Ron Asheton (bass, gtr, vocals), Scott Asheton (drums), Dave Alexander (bass), John Cale (viola, production).

Famously signed to the same label as the Doors in a joint deal that also secured the services of their Detroit contemporaries the MC5, the Stooges had by 1969 clearly outgrown their garage band "Louie, Louie" roots. In Iggy Pop, they possessed a shaman, psychedelic explorer and good old-fashioned showman to tower over Jim Morrison. When it came to an appetite for self-destruction, Dave, Ron and Scott were no slouches either. By rights, John Cale's credits should include "ringmaster" for his work in marshalling the band.

At times tightly coiled, at others, stoned, loose and on the verge of passing out, **The Stooges** has become an accepted classic not simply because of its enormous influence on punk, but also due to its refreshing sense of being uncluttered by excessive thought. Despite the endless free-rock workouts, full of tormented saxophone, in their live set, the Stooges were clearly happiest with tunes of three chords, 4/4 beats, and a structure of verse, chorus, verse. At a time when the golden age of psychedelia was already being obscured by the obsessive complexities of progressive rock, the Stooges turned music in a dark, early-glam direction, towards an unhealthy fascination with physical beauty, hard drugs and having a good time whatever the cost.

Part of the appeal of rock'n'roll has always been its presentation of a bad example. The Stooges were the embodiment of every right-thinking parent's worst dream. Even the cover pictures – the front gang-like, the back a police line-up – showed that the band had gone way beyond hand-holding and soda-pop.

Though most of the tracks on *The Stooges* have been covered at one time or another, it was the Sex Pistols' version of No Fun and the Damned's 1969 that broke the Stooges to a wider UK audience, resurrecting Iggy's solo career and going on to earn him the status of "grand Old Man Of Punk". When the album was recorded, however, Iggy and the band were in their roaring, early-twenties prime. Spitting dumb insolence, it sounds great from beginning to end.

Not Right, the first cut on the original vinyl release, is a declaration of everything the band stood for. Virtually incoherent, Iggy stumbles his way through the lyrics (essentially the story of a girl and Iggy himself, both of whom are "not right" for some unspecified, but easy to guess, reason), while Ron beats out a percussive chord riff and Dave and Scott chime in as and when they can. This air of strung-out despair and disillusion is also seen in the lengthy, chanted We Will Fall and love-gone-wrong-song Ann. The air is repeatedly cleared, though, by wide-eyed raging anthems driven by speed and testosterone such as "1969", Little Doll (a touching tale of barely controlled lust) and Real Cool Time. The lyrics of the latter are such a perfect rendition of adolescent conversation that they could have been transcribed from a phone call from Iggy to a girlfriend.

Two songs stand out above all others. "No Fun" catalogues the depressingly limited options that remain when you're constricted by poverty, boredom or drug abuse, gaining in power through the sheer inarticulate energy of the lyrics, not to mention one of the everlastingly transcendent guitar riffs of rock-'n'roll history. That shares the honours with I Wanna Be Your Dog, driven by a frantic repeated piano chord – one of Cale's trademarks – which can claim to have opened a world of transgressive sex and degradation to an essentially white-bread teenaged audience.

➲ We almost chose **Metallic KO**, Jungle, 1999

# 89

# Suicide

## Suicide

Red Star, 1977

Alan Vega (vocals), Martin Rev (synthesizer, multi-instruments, electronics).

One of the most important recordings in the development of electronic music, Suicide's eponymous album, **Suicide**, was responsible, in part, for the "democratization" of the synthesizer, drum machine and sampler. It took tools that had, until then, been used exclusively by serious classical composers and by the more cerebral of the progressive rock contingent, and placed them in the hands of pop groups.

The New York art-world cynicism of Alan Vega delivered images of speed and death that harked back to the early-Sixties school of death pop, and such timeless classics as "Dead Man's Curve" and "Leader Of The Pack". Backed entirely by electronically generated sounds from Martin Rev's self-created "Instrument" (a box of effects centred on a broken-up Farfisa organ), Suicide built a totally new kind of sound, with a soul of its own, which did not depend on the traditional stomp of rock. In a precursor of the house and techno movements, their energy derived instead from the rapid repetition of slowly evolving electronic phrases.

Suicide's music was a far cry from the later twinklings of happy hardcore, however, being a dark brew of Vega's psychedelic imagery and echoed yelps that stewed amid pulsing keyboard patterns and insistent machine-assembled drumbeats. Tracks like Rocket USA and Johnny subvert the wild, leather-jacketed genre of teenage pop, using the familiar motorcycle rhythm to transmit images of love, longing, death and despair. Johnny's "cruising the night and looking for love" that dare not speak its name, while "Riding around in my Chevy 69 . . . speeding along the Skyway" seems cool enough until we learn that "it's doomsday", and we're "riding along in a killer's car".

Though sharing a fascination with cars, speed and travel with mid-Seventies contemporaries Kraftwerk and Bowie, Suicide always aimed for the gut. Kraftwerk's lyrics might as well have been sung by Robbie the Robot, but Vega's reverbed-to-the-limit muttering and melodramatic screams sound on the brink of some shuddering revelation. On Cheree – a "Be My Baby" for Rev's synthesized wall of sound, with a delicate, innocent melody – Vega whispers words of love at mattress level, while at the climax to Girl he matches the sexual intensity of Jim Morrison, out-faking even the twelve-inch remix of Donna Summer's "Love To Love You Baby".

On an album of consistently distorted voice effects, Frankie Teardrop features the most twisted and disturbing vocals of all. Snapshot images, sometimes shockingly detailed, reveal that although Frankie's working all hours, he can't make enough money. About to be evicted, he cracks and kills his wife and children before turning the gun fatally on himself. Just when things can't get any worse, we follow Frankie, accompanied by frightening effects like corrugated iron being dragged across rough concrete flooring, down to Hell. The horror-movie ending – Frankie's alive in Hell, we're all Frankie, and we're all lying in Hell – leaves the listener feeling hollow and drained.

The final track, Che, opens with four funereal, doom-swathed organ notes that identify it instantly as a requiem, but Suicide's treatment of this hitherto sacrosanct form of tribute does anything but praise its subject. Once disentangled from the Gothic cathedral-style echoes, the lyrics turn out to be Ramones-level doggerel – "red star" is rhymed with "cigar", and we're told "they said he was a saint, I know he ain't" – that are every bit as punk rock as any of Suicide's peers.

⊃ We almost chose **Half Alive**, ROIR, 1981

# 90

# T Rex

## Electric Warrior

EMI, 1971

Marc Bolan (vocals, gtr), Mickey Finn (vocals, pcn), Steve Currie (bass), Bill Legend (drums), Rick Wakeman (kbds), Burt Collins (horns), Howard Kaylan / Mark Volman, aka Flo & Eddie (backing vocals), Ian McDonald (sax), Tony Visconti (pno, producer).

More than thirty years ago, Tyrannosaurus Rex stalked the Earth, a hippy duo Marc Bolan (Mark Feld) and Mickey Finn – carrying a set of bongos and an acoustic guitar, and wearing a cheesecloth shirt and crushed velvet loon pants. When this prehistoric version – a favourite of the immensely influential DJ John Peel and denizens of London's groovier underground clubs – was rendered extinct by Bolan's unquenchable thirst for stardom, the old dinosaur was replaced by a leaner, meaner carnivore with teen appeal and a sackload of glittery makeup. The six-syllable monicker disappeared in the few months in 1970 that came between the chart-topping singles "Ride A White Swan" and "Hot Love". T Rex emerged, kitted out with top-of-the-range equipment and a flash new image that out-camped Bowie, and finished the year with Get It On (released as the frankly more dubious-sounding "Bang A Gong" in the USA) going to the top ten on both sides of the Atlantic.

**Electric Warrior** was the first proper T Rex album; their earlier eponymous release, recorded by Bolan and Finn alone, comprised what seemed to be leftovers from the hippy dinosaur era. *Electric Warrior* was a teenage pop phenomenon, selling thousands in a market traditionally more disposed towards buying singles. All competent musicians in their own right, T Rex were working alongside one of Britain's most highly regarded producers, Tony Visconti, and had the services of star-quality sessionmen to call on. The album was an irresistible manifesto for the adoption of sleazy, boogie-based guitar rock, delivered in a wave of greasepaint, rhinestones and eyeliner, and pointing the way for a generation's worth of gender-blurring, dressed-up, fun music, from the New York Dolls to Kiss.

Bolan played ruthlessly on his double persona as the innocent slut, a winsome unthreatening smile for the cameras being ripped away as he let out guttural roars of impenetrably phrased desire and release. Smirking down from the bedroom walls of the UK, Bolan stole shamelessly from the Presley / Jagger book on sexual projection, and dressed it up as an innocuous alternative to David Cassidy or the Osmonds. When the gorgeous Marc and Mickey show hit the road, almighty rhythm section in tow, a predictable outbreak of T Rextacy swept the nation. The fires were further stoked by their next single, Jeepster.

Their music was never intended to last – there are no moving, epic tragedies of the human condition to be had here – but from the greasy riff that opens Mambo Sun, to the final crystalline cymbal crash of Rip Off, Electric Warrior is a total blast. With a basic philosophy that guitars are loud and are there for playing powerchords, some of rock's most powerful musical hooks, and an affection for the simplest of bass and drum boogie, it's an early-Seventies classic, coke-fuelled, trashy but immaculate, and still a great record for bopping, posing and dancing.

More than twenty years after Bolan's tragic death in a road accident – all the more poignant for happening when he was on the verge of regaining his superstar status in the UK after an ill-advised move to the US – T Rex have become a cult. Despite all the showmanship, and the shamelessly meaningless lyrics, squeezed out still wet with lust, Electric Warrior can't be written off as ephemeral pop. Punk bands, much of the new wave and a whole swathe of hard-rocking indie types owe a hell of a lot to the swaggering Mark Feld, the man who brought feather boas back to the dancehalls.

➲ We almost chose **Slider**, 1972, EMI

# 91

# Talking Heads

## Remain In Light

Sire, 1980

David Byrne (vocals, gtr, bass, kbds, pcn), Chris Frantz (drums, kbds, pcn), Tina Weymouth (bass, kbds), Jerry Harrison (gtr, bass, kbds), Eno (bass, kbds, vocals), Adrian Belew (gtr), Jose Rossy (pcn), Robert Palmer (pcn), Nona Hendryx (vocals).

As the Seventies gave way to the Eighties, New York City was the hippest place in the music world, and Talking Heads were the coolest band in the city. Out in Hicksville, all the intelligentsia were dancing to their whiter-than-white, antsy neo-funk. Byrne, Frantz and Weymouth had been together since design school on Rhode Island, and had paid their dues living in a Lower East Side loft. They'd drafted Harvard grad and former Modern Lover Harrison in 1977, and formed an enduring alliance with Brian Eno on their first visit to the UK the following year. Riding the new wave without ever descending to the gut level of punk rock, they helped establish the art-core New York sound that would lead into the No Wave noise experiments of the Eighties.

For **Remain in Light**, the four full-time Heads were able to draw on a fearsomely impressive team of musical support. They also called on Eno, who had produced their last two albums, to share the songwriting. The resulting nervous, disjointed funk masterpiece, in particular the standout track Once In A Lifetime – released as a single, and an early MTV video hit – propelled the band to stardom. *Remain in Light* had a profound effect on rock music at the start of the Eighties, encouraging experimentation with polyrhythm, electronics and previously untried instruments, and it also marked the start of Byrne's own interest in world music.

**Born Under Punches** bursts into life with frantic, distorted guitar lines, a twisted funk beat, and anxious lead vocals that contrast wildly with, and are barely held in check by, the soothing, encouraging voices of the chorus. Someone trots out a slick, if tense, patter like a hyped-up con artist; others chant; and a slurring, trance-like presence declares that "drowning cannot hurt a man, fire cannot hurt a man". This disturbing hint of religious ecstasy, possession and trance-induced wisdom is echoed throughout the album, from the urgent, sex-as-devotion, worship of an ill-defined "she" in **The Great Curve** to the churchy call-and-response chorus of **Houses In Motion**. Elsewhere, as in **Crosseyed And Painless**, the funk turns jagged and menacing under Eno's warped supervision, while the lyrics swim with ominous imagery or deranged, pointless rap.

"Once In A Lifetime" – lost in a modern world – and **Houses In Motion** – a confessional, swampy funk number – reel with self-doubt and paranoia, while self-image collapses entirely in **Seen And Not Seen**, a self-contained short story of identity crisis.

The two final cuts are, however, the most intriguing. **Listening Wind** is almost unique in North American music in presenting a sympathetic view of a freedom fighter, Mojique – from some unspecified country – struggling against US domination. With its non-European rhythms and a restrained Eno adding a ghostly atmosphere, it depicts the wind as representing the spirit of a people. **The Overlord** grinds along like some droning juggernaut, gaining in power through its measured, irresistible pace, with Byrne intoning about collapse and decay. In fact, all the songs on **Remain In Light** writhe with insecurity, as multiple voices and multiple points of view jostle to be heard. The music turns away from the rock tradition to take a global perspective, calling on new beats and defining a new vision based on the unsettling questioning of accepted values.

➲ We almost chose **Fear of Music**, Sire, 1979

# 92

# Television

## Marquee Moon

Elektra, 1977

Tom Verlaine (gtr, kbds, vocals), Richard Lloyd (gtr, vocals), Billy Ficca (drums), Fred Smith (bass, vocals).

The mid-Seventies were a grim time for rock fans. By and large, the young guns of the Sixties had transformed into aloof rock gods bloated by wealth and drugs, while the music had drifted towards terminal self-indulgence, with the conceits of Emerson, Lake and Palmer, Yes, and their ilk being treated as visionary. Then along came a new wave of gunslingers from the small clubs in New York, to cut through the crap and give rock'n'roll a new lease of life.

The city's new wave encompassed snotty three-chord wonders who yelled rock'n'roll rebellion in two minutes of shambolic petulance; painters, poets, and performance artists; and more thoughtful bands such as Television, whose staccato rhythms, off-key vocals and metallic, postmodern productions had little in common with the lush Californian sounds then dominating the FM airwaves. Following a line that ran directly from the Velvet Underground by way of Patti Smith, Television carried forward the cerebral strand of the avant-garde in NYC.

The earliest incarnation of the band saw Verlaine trading guitar licks and junkie-poses with arch-nihilist Richard Hell, but Hell had moved on by the time **Marquee Moon**, the first Television album, arrived in 1977 like a breath of fresh air. OK, there were occasional echoes of choice hippy forebears – Love, the Byrds, Beefheart, and the meandering guitar solos of Jerry

Garcia or Neil Young (especially on the ten-minute Marquee Moon itself) – but most of the album was genuinely new and different. There was nothing warm and soulful about it at all – here was the discordant sound of alienation, and it had pretensions to art. Nick Kent, in the *NME*, hailed it as "a 24-carat inspired work of genius", but despite critical slavering, it only reached number 28 in the UK, and failed to chart in the US.

Television had been honing their skills for some years. Verlaine – born Tom Miller, he had unpretentiously re-named himself after the French poet – was a Coltrane-obsessed free-form jazz fan, who found a perfect foil in the more disciplined approach of fellow guitarist Richard Lloyd. Since appearing on Patti Smith's debut single "Hey Joe", Verlaine had developed an aggressively dexterous soloing style and a surreal line in enigmatic lyrics. Drummer Billy Ficca had been with the band since they were the Neon Boys, while bassist Fred "Sonic" Smith, who replaced Richard Hell, was a former member of the MC5. Together, said *NME*, they were like "a fist punching metal rivets of sound".

In May 1977, Television toured the album in the UK, supported by fellow CBGB stalwarts Blondie, and confounded expectations by encoring with "Jumpin' Jack Flash". Twelve months later, they released their second album, *Adventure*, which seemed comparatively short of ideas. To all impressions burned out, the band split within months. Verlaine pursued a solo career with a minor cult following, until re-forming the band for the one-off *Television* album in 1994. Its failure to chart on either side of the Atlantic eventually caused the band to split again.

*Marquee Moon* influenced virtually everyone who emerged from the new-wave scene, whether other CBGB veterans like Talking Heads, second wavers like R.E.M. (who frequently cover See No Evil on stage), or British stars like Elvis Costello and Echo and the Bunnymen. Uniquely, it flew the flag for guitar virtuosity at a time when instrumental prowess was deeply unfashionable. its complex structures suggesting that perhaps the Blank Generation was not so blank after all.

➲ We almost chose **Adventure**, 1978

# 93

# Tortoise

## Millions Now Living Will Never Die

Thrill Jockey/City Slang, 1996

Doug McCombs (bass), John Herndon (drums, synths, vibes), John McEntire (drums, synths, vibes), Dave Pajo (gtr), Dan Bitney (synths, pcn).

Tortoise are the ultimate practitioners of what has been labelled "post-rock" – lyric-free, abstract constructions of mood-creating sounds. To a large extent, they have dispensed with the time-honoured notion of the rock "song" in favour of extended presentations of looser pieces with an improvised feel. Kicking off in Chicago in 1990, they draw on the groundbreaking late-Eighties work of Slint (as heard on *Tweez*, on Touch & Go), creating cavernous, echoing spaces linked by fiercely abrasive fragments of hard, mechanical noise. Masters of studio techniques and technology, their work reflects the Seventies heyday of Jamaican dub reggae as much as the cutting-edge scenes of the late Nineties. Adding a host of keyboards and electronic trickery to the basic "drums'n'guitars" line-up, they have torn away all the posturing and teenage angst of rock, to leave the sleek, at times mechanical, skeleton behind. Nonetheless, their music retains a warm, "human" feel.

For **Millions Now Living Will Never Die**, their second full-length recording, the band looked even more deeply into themselves than they had on 1994's *Tortoise*. The result was a piece of work with all the technical proficiency of jazz-rock fusion or progressive rock, but none of the associated pomposity. The 21-minute opening cut, Djed, evolves from a gently swaying bass and guitar groove into a series of differently textured "rooms", linked by percussion or staccato keyboard effects. As the piece slides between such extremes as looped, echoing vibraphone riffs, sparkling cascades of synthesized beauty, and stark electro-percussion, extra atmosphere is poured on by means of "found sounds", tape effects and electronic deconstructions. Continuously re-forming itself, with passages of tranquillity sandwiched between throbbing slabs of bass, "Djed" succeeds in keeping the listener enthralled throughout its mammoth length.

Elsewhere, as in the four-part Glass Museum, the experiment leans towards early Tangerine Dream, with a first "movement" of different time-signatures and swells of music that retreat, ocean-like, to leave a slow, considered, guitar melody. Notes softly dripping, one by one, the track balances on a sweet, vibraphone-led backing. Following a dramatic prog-rock second section, and a lightning-fast bongo-jazz third part, it returns to the original theme for the finale. The Taut And The Tame, for which previous Tortoise guitarist Bundy K Brown receives partial credit, is reminiscent of Yes, with tight, chopped chords, frenetic chase-scene drumming and a heart-racing bassline. The slow guitar solo, A Survey, by contrast, is laid over a gentle bassline and immersed in the whisperings of rainforest insect life.

Dear Grandma And Grandpa begins with a section of organ music from outer space, blooms into a deep, pulsing bass coloured with distorted radio transmissions from astronauts unknown, then transmutes further into a chain of echoing synth moods. It runs seamlessly into Along The Banks, which opens with a menacing spy-movie guitar line before itself growing and changing, first into a sloppy, night-club-jazz drum riff, with a spacey, slide-guitar theme, then back to movie espionage, to close the album.

Dinner party music for the avant-garde maybe, but Tortoise are undeniably among the most intriguing musical practitioners of the Nineties. Their impeccable musical tastes and technical ability are highlighted by their minimalist blend of Krautrock, dub and tasteful jazz.

➲ We almost chose **TNT**, 1998

# 94

# Tricky

## Maxinquaye

Fourth & Broadway, 1995

Tricky (vocals), Martina (vocals), Pete Briquette (bass), James Stevenson (gtr), Tony Wrafter (flute), FTV (gtr, drums), Allison Goldfrapp (vocals), Ragga (vocals), Mark Saunders (kbds, producer).

Epic, multi-layered, and ever eager to mess with your mind, Tricky's music challenges and engages like no other product of the Nineties. As a rule, Bristol's street thugs are not renowned for their eloquence, but then Adrian Thaws, the Tricky Kid, has always been the exception. Most gang-running young men put behind bars don't combine screw-face braggadocio with a taste for cross-dressing; fewer still go on to record platinum solo albums. Combining a prodigious appetite for marijuana with a disturbing morbidity, Tricky filled **Maxinquaye** from a grab bag of influences, to define his uniquely bleak and depressing take on trip-hop, and create one of the most enduring recordings of recent times.

Darker than contemporaries Portishead, and feeling no compulsion to please the party-going crowd, Tricky's skunk-smoking paranoia and eclectic sampling pushed the Bristol sound into a different gear. Using eerie orchestral samples as percussion, lifting fragments from sources as disparate as Shakespear's Sister, the Chantelles, and the Smashing Pumpkins, and completely re-writing the book on the young urban black male image, he set about building a new sound from the ground up.

Tricky's first involvement with music came with the Wild Bunch, the DJ/Soundsystem collective that went on to spawn Massive Attack. Moving away from the bad-boy world, he grew more immersed in making his own music, working on a series of powerful if unsettling raps and providing atmospheric guest vocals for the first two Massive Attack albums, *Blue Lines* and *Protection*.

Shortly afterwards, he met, and started working with, his female muse and partner, the mysterious Martina. When his first recording with her, Aftermath, was rejected by Massive, Tricky decided to go solo. Martina's soul-diva stylings combine with his own singing on all eleven tracks of *Maxinquaye*.

The stifling climate of claustrophobia, dysfunction and gender-confusion that permeates the entire album is already apparent on the sleeve, which shows the couple in wedding garb – Tricky in a white lace dress, Martina suited in top hat and tails. It's encapsulated by cuts such as Suffocated Love, which repeatedly hints at sexual insecurity and lust, and the slow, even-paced, but far from mellow Abbaon Fat Tracks, with its "Fuck you in, tuck you in, suck you in" lyrics.

All through the album, male and female roles are continually exchanged. Martina even takes lead vocals on the uber-male Black Steel, which illustrates the stark choice between compulsory military service and jail. Previously the exclusive, hard-core property of Public Enemy, it gains a new poignancy through Martina's defiant singing. Her voice also shines on the slow, bluesy Pumpkin and the shimmering echoes of Aftermath.

With the exception of the exuberantly malicious Brand New / You're Retro, in which Tricky gleefully disses the competition and leaves them breathing his dust, *Maxinquaye* reeks of self-doubt and reappraised self-image. From the staggering booze'n'puff disaster of Ponderosa to the stuttering protest of You Don't, he picks open his more troubling character traits and explores them. By the final track, Feed Me, where sampled sounds include a pistol being cocked and an irregularly spaced, torture-like dripping, the disjointed rhythms and asthmatic vocals reveal a mind struggling to remain sane.

◗ We almost chose **Pre-Millennium Tension**, PolyGram, 1996

# he Velvet Underground

## he Velvet Underground

erve, 1969

u Reed (vocals, gtr, kbds), Maureen "Mo" Tucker (bass, pcn, drums, vocals),
erling Morrison (gtr, vocals), Doug Yule (organ, bass, gtr, drums, kbds, vocals).

Once they'd successfully claimed the high ground as spokesband for the freaks of the world, then wriggled their way out of Andy Warhol's clammy grasp, the Velvet Underground had time to stop shouting and get a little sleep. Despite the echoes of their first two albums, which would rumble on for the next three decades, not until their third album, **The Velvet Underground**, did the band truly explore a spiritual direction, and while work up the light and shade in their music. Their previous release, *White Light/White Heat*, had closed with the non-verbal blazing row of "Sister Ray", a one-take stand-up ght using amplifier volume as the chosen weapon. John Cale's assive organ had eventually swung the day but he'd lost the war. y the time they returned to the studio, John Cale was pursuing a olo career, Doug Yule (who could play anything with strings on ) was in his chair, and Lou was penning intricately beautiful ongs such as Jesus – a subject far removed from the darkside ruggery that had characterized them to most commentators.

Even so, the album has an air of dissipated exhaustion, as if loving away from the frenetic atmosphere in the Factory had nabled the Velvets finally to stop getting all their calories from rystal meth. The music still holds almost intolerable tension, but 's played more slowly; the vocals are even more monotonous, ie chords drawn out for even longer. Although it's never safe to read too much into Lou's lyrics, the band still delicately champions the misfit and insists on a little toleration for the unusual.

Throughout the album, from opener Candy Says to penultimate track Murder Mystery, the lyrics come in fragmentary "found" dialogue, speed jive from Warhol superstars, snatches of love stories, and reported conversations. Like the confrontational literary experiments of William Burroughs, *The Velvet Underground* rewards repeated listening. Emphases change, information is gradually revealed, plays on words show themselves and different interpretations become possible. The music ranges from the delicate tracery of Pale Blue Eyes through the straight-up rocking of What Goes On to the stereo games of "Murder Mystery".

Elegant little touches such as the "doo doo wah" fade, sounding like the Chiffons after a hard night, at the end of "Candy Says"; the polite meshing of solos in "What Goes On"; and the overwhelming oceanic swells that punctuate I'm Set Free, show a prime rock'n'roll band at its creative peak. Reed's ear for dialogue and confident delivery enable him to recount intellectual kinkiness, justify hedonism, and tell us that "between thought and expression there lies a lifetime" in Some Kinda Love.

"Murder Mystery" may be riddled with images of death and domination, like some paedophile snuff movie conjured up in an emotionless nightmare, but there's rare purity and sincerity in the gentle looks at illicit love and reprehensible behaviour on "Pale Blue Eyes" and "Jesus", and catharsis, even redemption, in "I'm Set Free". If it hadn't been so drug-raddled, the album could be banging a tambourine for the Salvation Army.

The Velvets went on to become legendarily influential; the story goes that everyone who bought their first album on release went on to form a band. Certainly the louder, more extreme music of their early years can be seen as ancestral punk rock. This album, however, closing with Mo Tucker's unconventionally beautiful voice adding emotional depth to the otherwise trite lyrics of After Hours, is a gallery of beauty and terror.

➲ We almost chose **White Light/White Heat**, Verve, 1968

# 96

# Tom Waits

## Rain Dogs

Island, 1985

Tom Waits (gtr, kbds, vocals, producer), Robert Quine (gtr), Marc Ribot (gtr), Chris Spedding (gtr), Keith Richards (gtr, vocals), Ralph Carney (sax, wind), Larry Taylor (bass), Greg Cohen (bass), Mickey Curry (drums), Stephen Hodges (drums).

Ever since the Seventies, Tom Waits has been the singer-songwriter it's cool to like. One of the great innovators of rock, he's respected by fellow musicians as much as by the press and public; his songs have been covered by artists as diverse as Tim Buckley, Rod Stewart, Bruce Springsteen and the Eagles, and he even had Keith Richards contribute guest guitar and vocals on **Rain Dogs**.

From the mournful, country-influenced balladeer of his first two albums, through his bar-room bohemian late-Seventies persona, to his more theatrical vision of the Eighties and beyond, Waits has consistently written the songs to play when life turns to dirt. He'd been there, he understood and he had the whisky ready-poured. The sequence of *Swordfishtrombone* in 1983, *Rain Dogs* in 1985, and *Frank's Wild Years* in 1987, is generally recognized as his creative peak; *Rain Dogs* is a more fully realized, more consistent statement than the first, while avoiding the overdone stab at operetta that spoils the last of the trio.

*Rain Dogs* sees Waits unleash his unmistakable voice, with consummate skill and unwavering confidence, on a wide range of genres. Adult-oriented love songs include Hang Down; the folky, gentle Time; and Downtown Train, a ballad to "the girls", on which Tom wheezes out desire like Springsteen with emphysema. There's also Chandler-esque jazz-noir, as on 9th

**and Hennepin**, which revisits the unique voice so characteristic of 1976's *Small Change*, as well as short instrumentals like **Midtown**, the perfect soundtrack to a Sixties San Francisco car chase, and **Bride Of Rain Dog**, a far more unsettling collage of percussion, sax riffs and atonal harmonium.

A Southern Gothic atmosphere of richness in decay permeates the slow rockabilly of **Big Black Maria** and **Rain Dogs** itself. With its deranged accordion trilling, disjointed march beat, and edge-of-atonal guitar, that sound contrasts with the sly urban-whispering of **Clap Hands** – a nursery rhyme for cynical adults – and **Union Square**, a slow mutant rock'n'roll number that's all found percussion effects and shouted vocals.

Waits is at his most inspiring, however, when he brings his beat-generation rhythms and bright-lit flashes of broken imagery together with his arty Brecht-Weillian cabaret music. On tracks such as **Singapore**, with its cartoon-gnome march-pace, outlandish percussion and marimba melody; **Cemetery Polka**, a macabre tale of hatred, gossip and greed; and **Diamonds and Gold**, a mad-professor waltz of temptation and desire, he marshals restrained, sparse music and throwaway delivery to create songs that sound as though thrown together by a group of well-oiled friends in a clubhouse, late at night. The final track **Anywhere I Lay My Head**, brings the album to a roaring soul-revivalist, full-lunged close, stretching the blues to its limit with a brass band and harmonium drone and a disturbing New Orleans jazz-funeral coda.

*Rain Dogs* is a distillation of the epic North American music of the twentieth century, in which elements of jazz and blues flow alongside the sweetness of Broadway show tunes and the jarring dissonance of Captain Beefheart. Waits gibbers satisfying doom-filled observations on the foolishnesses of life, while Marc Ribot's blistering guitar adds counterpoint to his tobacco ravaged rasp. More original notions are explored within these nineteen tracks than most acts come up with in their entire careers.

⮑ We almost chose **Swordfishtrombones**, Island, 1993

# The Who

## Who's Next

Track/MCA, 1971; reissued with bonus tracks Polydor, 1995

Roger Daltrey (harp, vocals), Pete Townshend (gtr, organ, pno, kbds, vocals), Keith Moon (pcn, drums), John Entwistle (bass, pno, kbds, vocals, brass).

Over the course of the Sixties, the Who stumbled through one incarnation after another, from West London mods, by way of equipment-destroying pop heroes, to the rock-operatics of *Tommy*. Drained by his exertions on the saga of the "deaf, dumb and blind kid", Pete Townshend, the band's main creative force, knew that, while the fans would be kept briefly at bay by the *Live At Leeds* album, the pressure was on to come up with something even bigger and better.

Hence the Lifehouse project, a hugely ambitious and quintessentially early-Seventies scheme for a series of live performances, audience-participation happenings, and general multi-media experiments, designed to result in a double album and a movie. A few events actually took place, at London's Young Vic theatre, but the project as a whole – with Townshend a stressed-out drunk who needed absent manager Kit Lambert as a counterbalance, and the band riddled with drug abuse – fell apart.

To rescue something from the shreds of that "crazy and grandiose" dream, Lambert persuaded the band to relocate, first to New York, then to Stargrove (Mick Jagger's place in the country), and finally to Olympic Studios in London. There the obstinate Townshend hooked up with the equally hard-headed producer Glyn Johns. Between them they wrestled out **Who's Next**: a collection of nine brilliantly structured, wide-ranging songs that loses nothing whatsoever for the lack of a narrative thread to bind them together. The album went to the top of the UK charts, to number four in the US; set new standards for hard, heavy rocking; and furnished the band with the bulk of their live set for the rest of the decade.

The CD reissue of *Who's Next* includes an additional seven tracks recorded for the Lifehouse project, four of which are previously unreleased. Every track has been remastered, and the package comes with a 24-page booklet with full recording details and two essays; Townshend's inside story, and an informative piece by John Atkins, the editor of *Generations*, the Who fanzine.

From the groundbreaking synth patterns that open Baba O'Reilly to the crunching chords at the end of Won't Get Fooled Again – the original closing cut – *Who's Next* shows the band at their chest-beating wildest. Three-chord masterpieces change into jazzy, progressive grooves; there's a burst of gypsy fiddle here, hints of country music there; and classy, cool piano work from Nicky Hopkins adorns several tracks. Daltrey is equally adept at growling through the standard "girl I'm gonna make ya mine" poses, or musing with gentle sadness at the ways love can end. He tackles the good-times, on-the-road cruising of Going Mobile with pure joy, then gets tragic for Behind Blue Eyes. Townshend excels on "Baba O'Reilly", Bargain and Getting In Tune, shows his mastery of the effects pedals in "Going Mobile", and turns everything on full blast for the strutting "Won't Get Fooled Again". All "fighting in the street" and "meet the new boss, same as the old boss", that rallying cry to the masses may now sound lyrically dated, but it matches "Baba O'Reilly" for synth-loop experimentation and clashing guitar sounds, stretching out for more than eight minutes.

An impressive enough album in its original format, the new sixteen-track *Who's Next* now shines even brighter, bursting with rabble-rousing anthems, crazed drumming from the much-missed Keith Moon, clever and enormously strong bass, and Townshend's percussive, dangerous powerchord guitar.

➲ We almost chose **Meaty, Beaty, Big and Bouncy**, MCA, 1971

# 98

# Wire

## Pink Flag

Harvest, 1977

Colin Newman (vocals), Bruce Gilbert (gtr), Graham Lewis (bass), Robert Gotobed (drums).

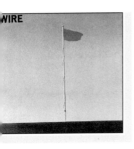

Signed to Harvest on the strength of two arrogant and well-executed tracks on the legendary *Live At The Roxy* compilation, Wire represented the more intelligent and coherent end of punk. Older, wiser and more experienced than most of their contemporaries, they combined art-school wit and invention with a refreshing, naive, punkish unfamiliarity with the subtleties of any of their instruments.

As demonstrated on their seminal debut, **Pink Flag**, Wire were masters of one-hit, concentrated doses of music; none of that "second verse, same as the first" nonsense for them. Despite their embrace of the concise snapshot aesthetic of punk, they had the ability to take a mature look at broader subjects, to experiment with imagery as well as plain chanted declamations, and to see the all-important fun in rock'n'roll. Though criticized at the time for their "progressive" outlook – on the second album, they went so far as to "pollute" their pure punk sound with synthesizers – it won them a wider audience than their contemporaries, and enabled them to survive, in one form or another, through to the Nineties.

Wire were every bit as capable of four to the floor, maximum velocity punk stompers as any of their peers. Reuters blunders along like some heavy-metal propaganda juggernaut, Brazil – featuring Newman's best stab at the Joey Ramone voice – is a madly positive, "get involved" rampage, and Surgeon's Girl riffs like crazy, boasts stupid lyrics, two chords and a drumbeat. Even hardcore anarchists Crass would have been pleased with Mr Suit, a tongue-in-cheek, obscenity-filled, anti-authoritarian rant. Most of the tracks on *Pink Flag*, however, aim a little higher, offering three or even four chords, more considered vocals and thought-provoking lyrics. Songs like 3 Girl Rhumba, Straight Line and Fragile variously explore strange kinds of lust and the total absence of desire, Start To Move hints at single-handed feats of adolescent sexual prowess, while Pink Flag has an enigmatic ambivalence about the very idea of love.

Elsewhere, as on the slow, grinding Lowdown and the Velvet Underground-ish Strange, they concentrate more on creating a mood than making a statement. "Strange" in particular, with a fuzzed-up guitar and simple no-frills drums, distils "Sister Ray" into less than four minutes of prickling tension and teen paranoia. 106 Beats That analyses an egocentric, Commercial is Wire's own instrumental surf-punk gem, and Mannequin – which opens mildly with "You're a waste of space" and then gets really bitter – totally shreds the beautiful but brain-dead hangers-on of punk, the ones who could never see behind the fashion. Both "Mannequin" and the anti-amphetamine stomper Champs share an ambitious, almost Dire Straits-like mood-elevating chord progression. Clever stuff, though it has to be said that it fails to match the virtually lyric-free, raging, three-chord beauty of 12XU, a true early-punk masterpiece.

On the CD reissue of *Pink Flag*, the original twenty-one tracks on the 1977 release have been boosted by two tracks from the following year: Dot Dash, a pro-speed late-night urban drive, and Options R. Though individual cuts do undoubtedly stand out, it's the cumulative effect of more than twenty short jabbing punches that makes *Pink Flag* one of the great rock albums. Wire showed a way for punk to move forward, while giving nothing away.

⊃ We almost chose **Chairs Missing**, EMI, 1978

# 99

# Robert Wyatt

## Rock Bottom

Virgin, 1974

Robert Wyatt (gtr, drums, kbds, vocals), Gary Windo (wind), Mike Oldfield (gtr), Ivor Cutler (kbds, vocals), Mongezi Feza (trumpet), Laurie Allen (drums), Alfreda Benge (vocals), Fred Frith (pno, viola), Hugh Hopper (bass), Richard Sinclair (bass).

Robert Wyatt was one of the great originators of English rock, gaining psychedelic street-cred with his Canterbury band Soft Machine, founder members of the British underground scene, and an equally impressive set of prog-rock campaign medals with Matching Mole. In both groups, Robert combined light jazz drumming with scatting, almost conversational vocals, unlike any other singer. On **Rock Bottom**, his first solo effort, he further extended the boundaries of rock singing into the impressionist zones of non-verbal communication, using the voice as both percussion instrument and creator of atmosphere. A master singer, Wyatt delighted in sharing his joy at the sheer range and richness of his instrument, but he also conveyed the broadest imaginable spectrum of emotions. When composing the record, he became paralysed following a fall from a window, and on the album he communicated his loss, fear, love, worship, awe, passion and desire with wordless yelps, gasps and drones.

Robert Wyatt's devotion to his craft had led him from performing note-perfect vocal renditions of Charlie Parker solos to the intense study of harmony, phrasing and rhythm. By confining recognizable lyrics to mere snatches, he encouraged listeners to construct their own references and create their own interpretations. Some of the album's unbearable poignancy can be attrib-

uted to his horrifying accident, but it's clear that he had planne
to trawl the most piercing emotions from the outset.

Sea Song, the gentle first track, opens with salty, maritim
images before introducing briny, enthusiastic drunken sex, hang
overs, stress and menstruation, demonstrating the "voice a
instrument" technique Wyatt developed during the So
Machine years in a long, trumpet-like, vocal reprise.

Two paired tracks, Little Red Riding Hood Hit Th
Road and Little Red Robin Hood Hit The Road, finishe
the first and second sides of the original vinyl album. The for
mer starts with a sobbing trumpet laid over a gently insisten
piano riff, and frightening vocal grunts of regret. Giving way t
"stop it" and "it hurts", the voice track is turned to play back
wards and joined by the piano; it's unsettling enough even befor
the couplet "So why did I hurt you? I didn't mean to hurt you"

Another pair of tracks, Alifib and Alifie – inspired by Alfie
Mrs Wyatt – open the second half. "Alifie", with its inspirationa
keyboards and panting, secretive vocals, is like making love at sun
rise. As pillow-personal as "Je T'aime", this is love as an act c
worship. Linking into "Alifib" by a part-meaningless rhyme, th
melody becomes twisted, with eerie squeals from a saxophone i
pain before redemption, in the form of Alfie herself, appears t
reprise the nonsense rhyme and to declare with touching devo
tion "I'm not your larder, I'm Alifie, your guarder".

A plaintive vocal refrain "can't you see them?" ends Roc
Bottom but loses its negative edge through sheer repetition, an
brings it to an almost upbeat conclusion. As it fades away
allowing Ivor Cutler and his harmonium to chant vaguely omi
nous threats, someone in the corner twitches a smile. By th
time the needle lifts from the groove, the room is filled wit
good humour and catharsis.

Wyatt's work since has wandered between revolutionary poli
tics, guest appearances and intense, microcosmic snapshots c
his own life. His voice illuminates anything it touches, but thi
is, quite simply, his greatest statement.

⮕ We almost chose **Nothing Can Stop Us**, Rough Trade, 1982

# 100

# Neil Young

## Tonight's The Night

Reprise, 1975

Neil Young (vocals, gtr, harmonica, pno, producer), Nils Lofgren (gtr, pno), Jack Nitzsche (gtr, kbds), Ben Keith (gtr), Kenneth A. Buttrey (drums), Tim Drummond (bass, drums), Ralph Molina (drums), Billy Talbot (bass), Danny Whitten (gtr).

Neil Young is known for folk-rock whose clear-spoken sincerity could bring a tear to the eye of an inner-city cop. He's also a feedback-wielding, guitar-skinning bastard rock'n'roller, responsible for launching an epidemic of tinnitus across the stadiums of the west. His solos and singing may be riddled with imperfections, but that just boosts the sense of overpowering conviction. Despite being the ultimate hippy with long hair and acoustic guitar, he was respectfully name-checked by Johnny Rotten and lauded as "Godfather Of Grunge". All these contradictions have their roots in **Tonight's The Night**.

Having paid his dues in a series of Canadian garage bands, Neil Young moved, via Buffalo Springfield and Crosby, Stills, Nash and Young, into the big league. By the start of the seventies, he was free both to develop his wistful acoustic leanings, and to indulge a taste for harder electric rock. Hooking up with LA bar band Crazy Horse in 1969, he recorded *Everybody Knows This Is Nowhere*, unveiling a new brand of majestic, stumbling rock on "Cinnamon Girl" and "Down By The River".

By 1973, when he cut *Tonight's The Night* – which was only released in 1975 – Young was a major star, thanks to *Harvest* and *After The Goldrush*. Like many of his West-coast musical contemporaries, he moved in circles rife with substance abuse.

Although Young had sung of "The Needle and the Damage Done" for some years, and had always steered clear of heroin himself, *Tonight's The Night* was a drunken, messed-up wake, the band's farewell to two of their fellow travellers who fatally overdosed within weeks of one another. Deliberately ragged around the edges, with the feel of a half-finished demo, it bridged the gap between Young's folk-tinged regret and his later, full-on electric-rock anger, eliciting sympathy for those who died and the pain felt by those who remain to mourn them.

Tonight's The Night itself (different versions of which open and close the album) tells the stories of Bruce Berry (roadie for CSN&Y) and Danny Whitten (Crazy Horse guitarist). Through the dope smoke, beer and who knows what, it's hard to read the emotions behind Young's wavering voice. Blending fear and celebration, the song builds up Berry as a damn nice guy before the shock lyric "I picked up the phone . . . heard that he died . . . out on the mainline" slams the door closed on his life.

Recorded too soon after the deaths for any readjustment to have set in, there's little brightness to be had. Speaking Out is drunken, paranoid boogie, Whitten himself makes a ghoulish cameo on Come On Baby Let's Go Downtown, and Tired Eyes shows a genuine affection for the losers, dopers and friends it recalls. With Roll Another Number, a perverse relish in one's own helplessness – "It's too dark to put the keys in my ignition / And the morning sun has yet to climb my hood ornament" – lurches into a fixed-grin, good-times singalong, but the mood disappears as abruptly as it appeared, leaving just the fixed, stoned, eyes-to-the-road stare of Albuquerque.

Swinging quietly from black depression to the brink of suicide and back, this intense and cathartic album stands as Young's finest hour. Not until 1979, however, with *Rust Never Sleeps* and *Live Rust*, did he regain mainstream respect. He then spent the Eighties back in the wasteland, only to resurface in 1989 – grizzled, incredibly loud and thoroughly pissed off – with *Freedom*. Since then, the old feller's never looked back.

➲ We almost chose **Arc/Weld**, Reprise, 1991